DATE DUE

THE WAY OF
THE WARRIOR

✛

This volume is one of a series that chronicles the history and culture of the Native Americans. Other books in the series include:

THE FIRST AMERICANS
THE SPIRIT WORLD
THE EUROPEAN CHALLENGE
PEOPLE OF THE DESERT

The Cover: Sioux warriors ride in battle on brightly colored mounts in this detail from an 1884 drawing attributed to New Bear, a Hidatsa artist. The introduction of the horse by Spanish explorers in the 17th century changed both the motives and methods of warfare for Indians of the Great Plains.

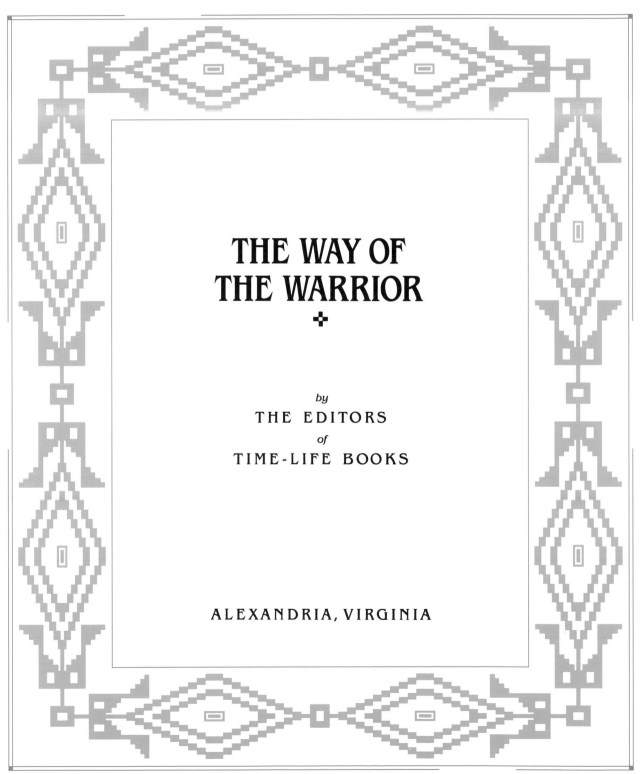

THE WAY OF
THE WARRIOR

✦

by
THE EDITORS
of
TIME-LIFE BOOKS

ALEXANDRIA, VIRGINIA

TIME-LIFE BOOKS

EDITOR-IN-CHIEF: Thomas H. Flaherty
Director of Editorial Resources: Elise D. Ritter-Clough
Executive Art Director: Ellen Robling
Director of Photography and Research: John Conrad Weiser
Editorial Board: Dale M. Brown, Janet Cave, Roberta Conlan, Robert Doyle, Laura Foreman, Jim Hicks, Rita Thievon Mullin, Henry Woodhead
Assistant Director of Editorial Resources: Norma E. Shaw

PRESIDENT: John D. Hall

Vice President and Director of Marketing: Nancy K. Jones
Editorial Director: Russell B. Adams, Jr.
Director of Production Services: Robert N. Carr
Production Manager: Marlene Zack
Supervisor of Quality Control: James King

Editorial Operations
Production: Celia Beattie
Library: Louise D. Forstall
Computer Composition: Deborah G. Tait (Manager), Monika D. Thayer, Janet Barnes Syring, Lillian Daniels
Interactive Media Specialist: Patti H. Cass

Time-Life Books is a division of Time Life Incorporated

PRESIDENT AND CEO: John M. Fahey, Jr.

THE AMERICAN INDIANS

SERIES EDITOR: Henry Woodhead
Administrative Editor: Jane Edwin

Editorial Staff for *The Way of the Warrior:*
Senior Art Directors: Dale Pollekoff, Herbert H. Quarmby
Picture Editor: Jane Coughran
Text Editors: Stephen G. Hyslop (principal), John Newton
Writers: Robin Currie, Maggie Debelius
Associate Editors/Research: Mary Helena McCarthy, Catherine Chase Tyson (principals), Marilyn Murphy Terrell
Assistant Art Director: Susan M. Gibas
Senior Copyeditor: Ann Lee Bruen
Picture Coordinator: David Beard
Editorial Assistant: Gemma Villanueva

Special Contributors: Ronald H. Bailey, William C. Davis, William C. Meadows, Peter Pocock, Lydia Preston, David S. Thomson (text); Martha Lee Beckington, Craig Chapin, Jennifer Veech (research); Barbara L. Klein (index).

Correspondents: Elisabeth Kraemer-Singh (Bonn), Christine Hinze (London), Christina Lieberman (New York), Maria Vincenza Aloisi (Paris), Ann Natanson (Rome). Valuable assistance was also provided by: Elizabeth Brown (New York), Carolyn L. Sackett (Seattle), Dick Berry (Tokyo).

Library of Congress Cataloging in Publication Data
The Way of the warrior/by the editors of Time-Life Books.
     p.   cm. — (The American Indians)
Includes bibliographical references and index.
ISBN 0-8094-9416-7
ISBN 0-8094-9417-5 (lib. bdg.)
     1. Indians of North America—Wars.   2. Indians of North America—Social life and customs.
I. Time-Life Books.   II. Series.
E81.W39   1993
399'.08997—dc20   92-22261
                                   CIP

CONTENTS

1
THE WELLSPRINGS OF CONFLICT
18

2
THE RITUAL OF WARFARE
74

3
THE TACTICS OF DECEPTION AND DARING
128

ESSAYS

A GALLERY OF FIGHTING MEN
6

CROWNING GLORIES
57

A HERO OF THE MANDAN NATION
66

FINDING HONOR IN THE MILITARY
110

REBIRTH OF THE BLACK LEGS
120

THE WEAPONS OF WAR
165

A GALLERY OF FIGHTING MEN

WHITE BELLY, SIOUX

TWO LEGGINGS, CROW

KEOKUK, SAUK AND MESQUAKIE

MANY ARROWS, NAVAJO

TWO HATCHET, KIOWA

WETSIT, ASSINIBOIN

RED WING, CROW

WAR EAGLE, IROQUOIS

UTSE-TAH-WAH-TI-AN-KA, OSAGE

WAR CAPTAIN, NAMBE PUEBLO

JAMES LONE ELK, SIOUX

KILL SPOTTED ELK, ASSINIBOIN

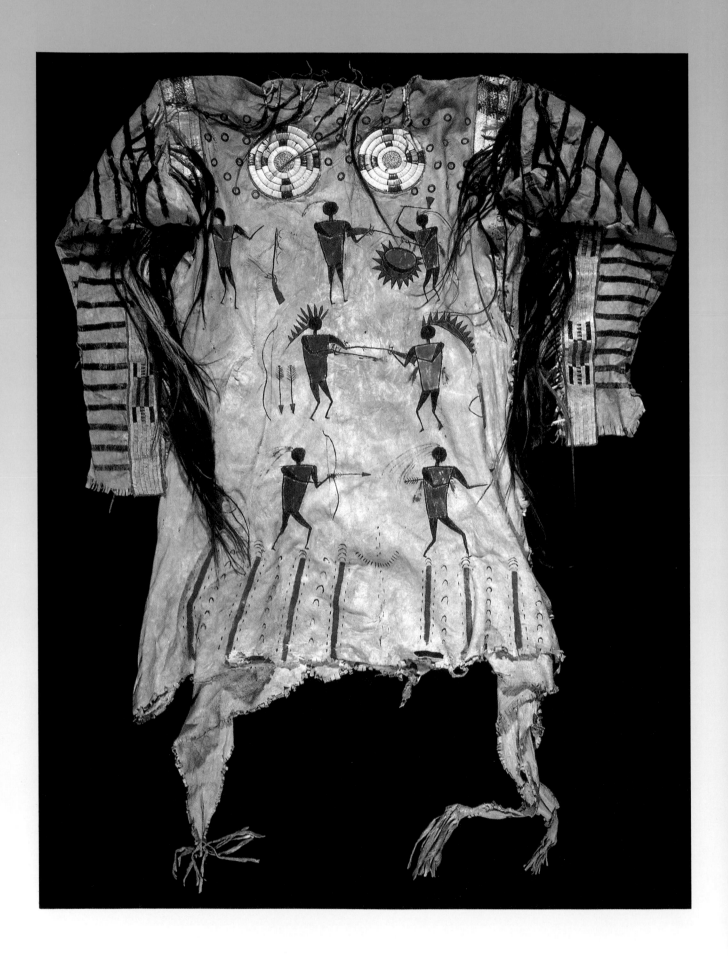

1

THE WELLSPRINGS OF CONFLICT

Drawings on a tunic that belonged to a 19th-century warrior from the northern Plains celebrate the owner (painted in red) and three of his successes in battle. Adorned with hair and porcupine quill medallions (top center), the leather garment was worn in war-related ceremonies rather than in combat.

In the late summer of 1857, a Quechan warrior who lived on the California bank of the lower Colorado River had a fateful dream. "I dreamed that I had all kinds of animals and birds around me on the mountain," he told his neighbors in the village of Algodones. "I laid hold of all these things and killed them." The warrior then cast about for help in interpreting his dream, asking opinions of fellow tribesmen on both sides of the river. His listeners assured him that the dream meant he would rise to great heights as a warrior and slay many enemies. But there were wider portents for the tribe as a whole. The man from Algodones could see only one way to fulfill his personal prophecy: He must lead the Quechan in battle against their traditional enemies to the east, the Maricopa.

This sudden and seemingly unprovoked resolution to go to war would not have come as a surprise to other American Indians. Like native peoples all across the continent, the Quechan regarded warfare as one of life's intrinsic challenges and prided themselves on being ready for battle at all times. For some groups, fighting was the principal pursuit after farming or hunting. Indeed, in Indian languages, the term for warrior was often the same as that for hunter. Nor was the apparent whimsy of the Quechan decision—the dream that inspired it—at all unusual. The Quechan, like most tribes, put great stock in dreams and let such visions influence them in war as in other vital matters.

The encounter that resulted from this dream would prove to be one of the last major battles between Indians in North America. Appropriately, it was fought with weapons of the sort Native Americans had relied on for centuries before Europeans introduced firearms to the New World. And the conflict was no less traditional in its meaning for the participants. From start to finish, it was bound up in rituals that provided the warriors with an incentive more powerful than any hope of material gain. As in other tribes, Quechan fighting men looked for guidance from the spirits, who spoke to them through dreams and other signs and directed them through the ordeal of battle, come victory or defeat. Although any

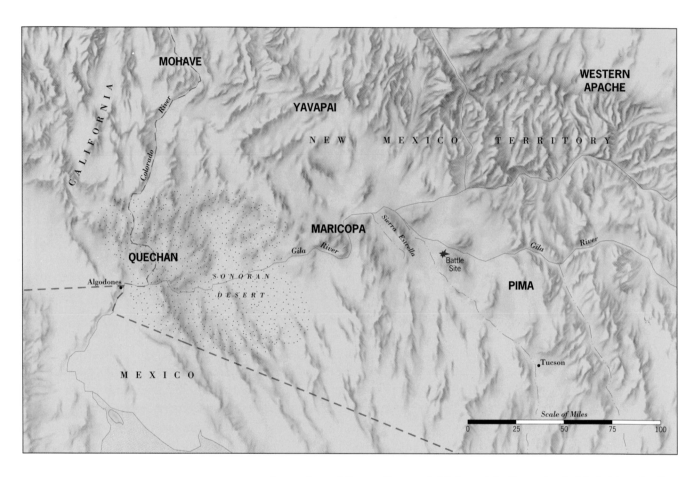

In the last significant confrontation between old and bitter rivals, the Quechan and their Mohave allies trekked eastward from their homeland on the Colorado River through the Sonoran Desert to mount a surprise attack on a Maricopa settlement along the Gila River on September 1, 1857. After enlisting the aid of their Pima neighbors, the Maricopa were able to rally their forces and engage the invaders in a pitched battle.

number of worldly motives might impel Indians to fight, taking to the warpath was ultimately an act of faith—a quest that put men in touch with unseen powers and gave them the strength to confront their destiny.

Although the Quechan and the Maricopa were culturally similar and spoke related Yuman languages, their rivalry reached back for generations. Here, as in other feuds between neighboring Indian tribes, competition for natural resources may have been the root cause of hostilities. The Maricopa—who farmed the banks of the Gila River east of its confluence with the Colorado—included among their ranks the descendants of people who had once lived next to the Quechan along the Colorado and may have vied with them for fertile riverside bottom lands before being forcibly evicted in the late 18th century. However the conflict originated, it was sustained by sheer mutual animosity. More than 150 miles of desolate country separated Quechan villages from the nearest Maricopa settlements, yet war parties had bridged the gap time and again. In recent decades, the enemies had clashed on at least 21 occasions—battles seemingly motivated by little more than a desire for revenge. In 1832 Quechans on a raiding party had been ambushed by Maricopas and massacred. The Quechan had retaliated the following year, and on it went. To preserve tribal pride and demonstrate tribal resolve, every attack had to be repaid in kind, every scalp lost had to be recouped. In such an atmosphere, warriors were often visited by violent dreams.

Both sides in this bitter rivalry had managed to maintain peaceful relations with other tribes in their vicinity. The Quechan had allied themselves with the Mohave, who lived farther north along the Colorado, while the Maricopa—a small tribe relative to the Quechan—had reached a similar accommodation with the populous Pima, who lived close by the Maricopa in several villages along the Gila River and its tributaries. As these alliances made clear, neither the Quechan nor the Maricopa were indiscriminately warlike, but they were caught in a bind of reciprocal hostility, and not even recent incursions by white frontiersmen and federal troops had diverted them from their blood feud.

As in other Indian disputes, the enmity between the archrivals was expressed through two types of fighting expeditions. The small raiding party typically consisted of a dozen or so warriors and might be instigated by young men restless for action, whose aim was simply to stir up mischief and make off with food, some horses, and perhaps a few captives. The major war party was a tribal affair, organized by an experienced war leader who often sought help from the tribe's allies and mustered hundreds of men to meet the enemy in a pitched battle. Such encounters were sometimes governed by an elaborate protocol. The attackers might be detected as they approached their target, or they might send warning of their impending assault. In such cases, the battle would often be delayed long enough for the opposing war leaders to bring up their forces and deploy them in a formal array. Each side would scratch a line in the dirt—as a dare and as a form of magical protection. Once the opposing formations had faced off behind the lines, champions would stride forward to exchange insults and trade the first blows. Then the opposing ranks would surge together in a ferocious melee.

Whether they met on such formal terms or in impromptu skirmishes, the Quechan and Maricopa were generally well matched. They employed similar weapons: the bow and arrow, the lance, and a short hardwood club that resembled a potato masher. Both tribes trained their boys to

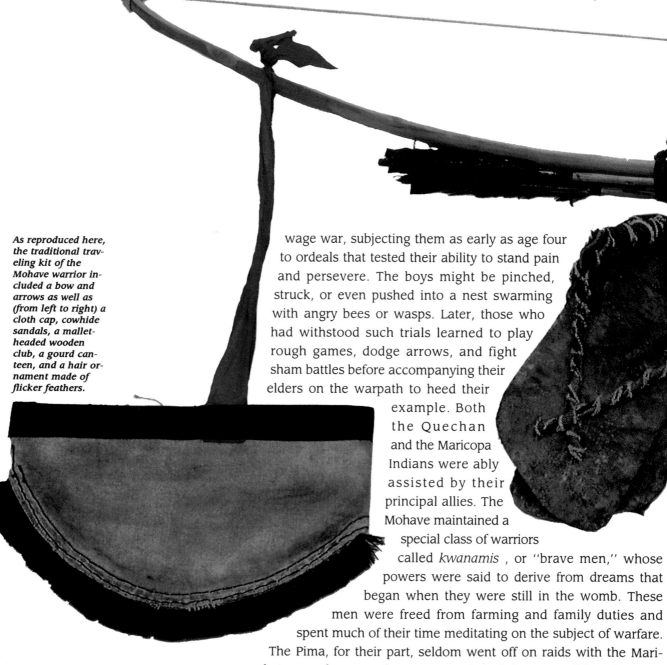

As reproduced here, the traditional traveling kit of the Mohave warrior included a bow and arrows as well as (from left to right) a cloth cap, cowhide sandals, a mallet-headed wooden club, a gourd canteen, and a hair ornament made of flicker feathers.

wage war, subjecting them as early as age four to ordeals that tested their ability to stand pain and persevere. The boys might be pinched, struck, or even pushed into a nest swarming with angry bees or wasps. Later, those who had withstood such trials learned to play rough games, dodge arrows, and fight sham battles before accompanying their elders on the warpath to heed their example. Both the Quechan and the Maricopa Indians were ably assisted by their principal allies. The Mohave maintained a special class of warriors called *kwanamis* , or ''brave men,'' whose powers were said to derive from dreams that began when they were still in the womb. These men were freed from farming and family duties and spent much of their time meditating on the subject of warfare.

The Pima, for their part, seldom went off on raids with the Maricopa but were always ready to come to their defense, conditioned as they were to guarding against the predations of their own traditional enemies to the north, the Yavapai and the Western Apache. Pima men, who liked to daub their hair with mud from the riverbed and twist it so that it dried in a helmetlike coiffure, looked fierce and acted accordingly, maintaining large herds of horses to ride against intruders.

Before an aspiring war leader could mount a campaign, he was expected to seek the approval of tribal elders. Quechan lore says that the Algodones man referred his dream to a *paxatan*, or ''civil leader,'' named

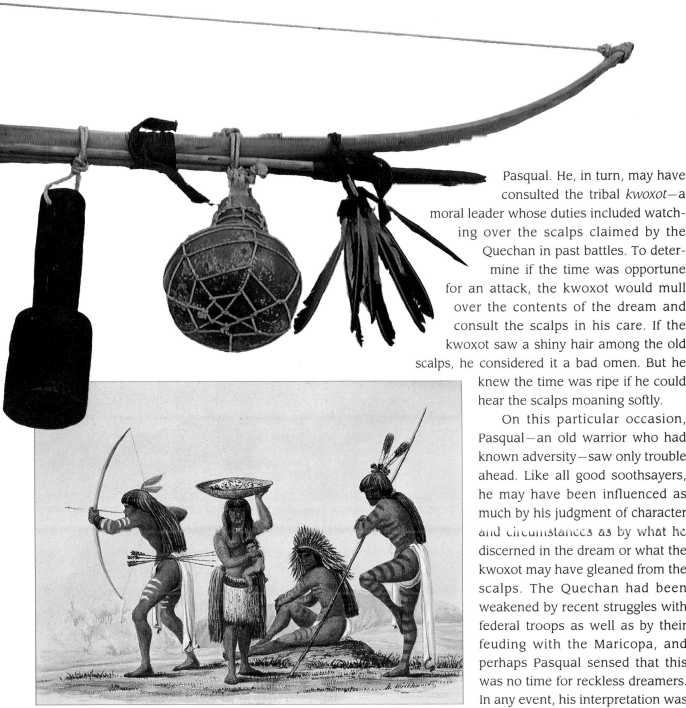

Three Mohave men pose with weapons while a woman attends to family duties in this 19th-century painting. The tribe supported dedicated warriors called kwanamis.

Pasqual. He, in turn, may have consulted the tribal *kwoxot*—a moral leader whose duties included watching over the scalps claimed by the Quechan in past battles. To determine if the time was opportune for an attack, the kwoxot would mull over the contents of the dream and consult the scalps in his care. If the kwoxot saw a shiny hair among the old scalps, he considered it a bad omen. But he knew the time was ripe if he could hear the scalps moaning softly.

On this particular occasion, Pasqual—an old warrior who had known adversity—saw only trouble ahead. Like all good soothsayers, he may have been influenced as much by his judgment of character and circumstances as by what he discerned in the dream or what the kwoxot may have gleaned from the scalps. The Quechan had been weakened by recent struggles with federal troops as well as by their feuding with the Maricopa, and perhaps Pasqual sensed that this was no time for reckless dreamers. In any event, his interpretation was discouraging in the extreme. "It means that you are going to die," he warned the man from Algodones after considering his dream, "and that all kinds of birds and animals are going to come and eat you."

Undeterred, the Algodones warrior pressed ahead and persuaded scores of Quechan fighting men to join him. Soon, his proposed attack won pledges of support not only from the tribe's close allies, the Mohave, but also from the Yavapai and the Western Apache, who resented the Maricopa for their alliance with the hostile Pima. Late in August 1857, the Quechan war party filed quietly out of the village without ceremony, song, or exhortation. Meanwhile, in the Mohave villages, the kwanamis and other warriors prepared themselves with a day and night of tribal dancing, during which women pranced around scalps taken in previous battles and the men sang to the accompaniment of a gourd rattle.

The various assault groups assembled at a rendezvous in the Sonoran Desert known as Parker, the first stage in their journey of nearly 160 miles. Theirs was the kind of large war expedition that the Mohave called *kawanatme* to distinguish it from small raiding parties. All together, there were several hundred warriors, all of them volunteers, variously equipped with bows, clubs, lances, and round rawhide shields.

Several healers accompanied them. Each specialized in treating a different kind of injury, from superficial arrow punctures to deep wounds from which the warrior's soul might escape and hover overhead, threatening to depart this world unless the healer intervened. Another medicine man came along to weave a spell that would lull the enemy into lethargy; he also scanned the horizon for omens such as a falling meteor or the sudden death of a deer.

One apparent omen manifested itself on the morning that the combined war party set out from Parker: An eagle soared through the air and then inexplicably dropped dead in front of the warriors. The Algodones warrior interpreted it as he had previous sightings of dying animals along the warpath—as confirmation that his dream was propitious and that their enemies would collapse before them. "We are great warriors," he reassured his comrades, "and everything favors us."

The trek across the bleak Sonoran Desert, with its sparse cover of creosote bush, bursage, and cactus, took about a week. The men traveled on foot rather than on horses because, more than a century after the animals' introduction to the region by the Spaniards, these tribes still lacked sufficient horses to assemble anything resembling cavalry. Accustomed to long periods of deprivation, each warrior carried only a small gourd canteen and a few handfuls of dried food.

After reaching Maricopa territory, the expedition made final preparations by donning war paint. The Quechans blackened their faces and drew a vertical red stripe down the center; they painted their hair red as

Dating from before the 1880s, a clay figurine wears the body paint and breechcloth of a Quechan man. Although similar effigies may have been used in funeral ceremonies for children, this type of pottery doll became popular as a trade item in the mid-19th century when white settlers arrived in Quechan territory.

well, and coiled it atop the head to form a kind of turban. The Mohaves, too, flaunted red hair, and daubed patterns of white zigzags, circles, lines, and spirals on their chests, with a horizontal black stripe across the face at eye level. On this occasion, no advance warning would be sent to challenge the enemy to a formal battle; these marauders hoped to surprise the Maricopas in their sleep. They would have to be extra stealthy, for years of feuding had left the Maricopa restless and watchful. "We were afraid to sleep late," a Maricopa warrior said of those days. "In the mornings, a coyote would howl and scare you: 'It is the Mohave; war is coming,' you thought, and you seized your bows."

This time, however, the Maricopa were caught off guard. Just before dawn on September 1, the attackers descended on one of two Maricopa villages, situated north of the Gila River some 30 miles south of present-day Phoenix. According to a Pima Indian named Owl Ear, who offered an account of the battle several decades later, the first victims were Maricopa women who were out early gathering mesquite beans. Assaults on women or children were not typical of Indian warfare, but they sometimes occurred when bitter enemies such as the Quechan and Maricopa crossed paths. Owl Ear recollected that the attackers "killed all the women except one, whom they kept to act as a guide. She was the sister of a well-known Maricopa warrior, and they compelled her to lead them to her brother's home. When they reached it, she was killed with a club and the man was chased, but he was as good a runner as he was a fighter, and they could not catch him." One of his pursuers shouted at him to "stop and die like a man, but he answered that if they could overtake him, he would show them how to die like a man." Such elusiveness was widely admired by Native American warriors, who saw nothing dishonorable in flight if it enabled a man to fight again from a position of strength.

All accounts agree that the attackers swiftly overran the Maricopa village. The hungry marauders ransacked the scattered, dome-shaped brush huts for food. They feasted on corn and black-eyed peas and, when they had had their fill, set the huts afire. Isaiah Woods, a United States mail superintendent who was camped less than a mile away, saw the columns of thick smoke rising from the huts and thought at first they were from signal fires. But as Woods reported in his journal, he and his white companions soon realized that they were at the scene of an Indian battle

Some 150 miles of unforgiving terrain, including the Kofa Mountains located in present-day Arizona, separated the Quechan and their allies from their enemies, the Maricopa. Going to war meant at least a week-long journey on foot with little more than the water collected in a gourd canteen and a bag of mesquite beans or other forage.

when an old Maricopa chief whose wife had been killed by the Quechan "rode furiously up to our camp, foaming at the mouth, and begged of us in good Spanish to aid them." Woods and the others declined, and the chief spurned them thereafter. "When the battle was over," Woods observed, "he refused to speak or understand a word of Spanish."

Leaving the village in flames, the attackers forded the river to track down the fleeing enemy. The ranks of the aggressors were noticeably diminished as they gathered on the south bank of the Gila near a pair of rocky prominences known as Pima Butte. Only 100 or so warriors remained, mostly Quechan. Reportedly, the rest fled either because they feared that they were about to be surrounded by the enemy, or because they saw forbidding omens, including a bleeding deer and a dead hawk.

Sometime around noon, the depleted Quechans were beset by several hundred Maricopas and Pimas, rallied from neighboring villages. One account says that the combatants paused long enough to engage in formalities. The two sides drew up in formation and sent forward challengers to boast and exchange insults. They accused each other of being not warriors but women. Then the carnage began.

Many of the Pimas were on horseback, and they bore down on the invaders with lances, sowing confusion and disarray. Foot soldiers followed. Arrows whistled through the air from both sides. They were tipped with points of flint or iron, some treated with rattlesnake venom or other poison to render them more lethal. At close quarters, however, the deadliest work was done by men wielding clubs. These instruments, carved from ironwood or mesquite, were pointed at one end for jabs to the body and had a large knob at the other end for blows to the head. For maximum effect, some men with clubs would grasp an opponent by the hair, pull his head down, and deliver a crushing blow from above or below.

Aside from such offensive weapons, certain Pimas carried rawhide shields painted in bright colors that reflected the sun and dazzled the enemy. "The shield carriers leaped nimbly about," a Pima warrior later explained, "twisting the shield constantly until, seen from the front, the disk presented an illusion of colors, making it a difficult target and a distraction to an opposing bowman."

Bolstered by their agile shield carriers and horsemen, the numerically superior Pimas and Maricopas proved unstoppable. Quechans and their remaining allies stood their ground courageously, and went down by the score—bodies pierced by lance and arrow, skulls fractured by clubs. A few survivors fled into nearby hills too steep for the Pima horses to follow and later made their arduous way back across the desert. When the struggle ended, the bodies of nearly 100 warriors, most of them Quechan, littered the plain near Pima Butte. "This was the bloodiest fight known," Owl Ear recollected, and indeed such a casualty count was exceptional for battles between Indians, which usually ended with the victors claiming a few scalps or carrying home perhaps a dozen captives. The vanquished Quechan, Owl Ear concluded, "came here to fight no more."

The triumphant Pimas and Maricopas took some scalps but otherwise left the fallen enemy to the coyotes and crows, refusing to handle the bodies for fear of catching the sickness that Indians in the region believed afflicted any foe. All the warriors who had killed or scalped opponents had to undergo an extended period of isolation. They fasted, sang, and bathed frequently in order to purify themselves of contamination. Only after many days did they emerge from isolation—an occasion marked by a victory dance. In this celebration women decorated with war paint mimicked the fighting men and heaped dirt and insults upon a scalp taken from one of the enemy dead.

The defeated side, meanwhile, mourned their dead in their own tribal ceremonies. For the Quechan, this meant elaborate rites that included the sacrifice of valued possessions such as horses and even houses. They burned so many cornfields that the commander of the U.S. Army fort in the area intervened out of concern that the tribe might become dependent on the federal government. Among the slain warriors mourned by the Quechan was the man from Algodones whose dream had led to the massacre at Pima Butte. Obeying tribal custom, the dead man's name was left unspoken, but his folly lives on in Quechan lore.

Although the battle at Pima Butte was unusually costly for the losing side, it was otherwise typical of the longstanding Native American tradition of tribal warfare. For countless generations before the arrival of Europeans, Indians had been energetically making war on their rivals. Of the hundreds of tribes that inhabited the continent, only a small portion lacked the will or means to organize military expeditions, and most of those groups were given to sparring or feuding on a lesser scale. Tribes of the arid Great Basin, for example, were too dispersed to form sizable raiding parties, but small numbers of them were known to waylay scattered individuals from rival tribes, steal their possessions, or carry off women. The northern Ojibwa of Canada generally

Three Quechan warriors pose for a photograph in the studio of E. A. Bonine around 1880. A U. S. Army officer who was posted on the western frontier in the mid-1800s commented that the Quechan "decorate themselves most splendidly for war. Their bodies are tattooed variously, according to their ideas of beauty or terrific effect."

avoided bloodshed, but cast spells on their enemies that were thought to be deadly. Some Inuit groups reversed the basic Indian pattern of directing violence outside the community and focused their aggression within the society. A survey of one such settlement in northern Canada found that every man 30 years of age or older had killed at least one of his fellows—usually in a dispute over a woman. Although the community as a whole tolerated such impulsive acts, it abhorred habitual killers and formed vigilante groups to track them down.

For the many tribes that did engage in formal combat with rival groups, war was a quite different affair from that practiced by Europeans. Tribes were too small to maintain standing armies, and a clash like that at Pima Butte, involving several hundred warriors, was considered major. Europeans who thought nothing of praying before going into battle expressed bewilderment and scorn at the mysticism that permeated the way of the warrior, from the purported magic of dreams and omens to the supernatural symbolism of war paint. For their part, most Indians found alien the European ideal of standing toe to toe on the battlefield until the last man fell. Like the Maricopa warrior who deftly eluded his assailants, they saw no disgrace in fleeing a hopeless fight or outmaneuvering their opponents through stealth, deception, and surprise.

White soldiers learned the hard way the value of Indian hit-and-run tactics. A Jamestown colonist described the unnerving prospect of hostile Indians "creeping on all fours, from the hills, like bears, with their bows

The stealth of Indian warriors was derived in part from their cunning as hunters, as shown in this engraving of a man disguised as a deer stalking prey along the upper Missouri. Europeans scorned such craftiness in war. One colonist complained that the Mohawk acted "more like wolves than men" and fought "in a secret, skulking manner."

in their mouths." Or as a Frenchman, employing other animal similes, said of his native foes: "They approach like foxes, fight like lions, and disappear like birds." Far from being insulted by such comparisons, Indian warriors proudly associated themselves with the strength and acumen of animals, whom they looked to for inspiration. American colonists who followed their example and learned to fight with predatory cunning helped wrest control of the colonies from a British army that ranked as one of the world's largest and best armed.

If whites came to appreciate and emulate the methods of Indian warriors, they remained puzzled by their motives. Prior to the time that Europeans made deep inroads on the continent, the Indians of North America rarely went to war to gain territory, simply because there was so much of it and because the concept of individual or tribal ownership of land had not yet taken root. To be sure, Indians occasionally fought for territorial hunting rights and for the acquisition of material assets such as food, weapons, captives, or tribute. In the Southeast, for example, the great chiefs of the mound-building Mississippian culture sometimes used force—or the threat of it—to compel outlying villages to provide them with goods or laborers. The object of thus extending the chief's domain was not simply to enrich the leader in this life, however, but to obtain materials and manpower for his elaborate funerary rites, which took place atop the mounds. Here, as among other Native American cultures, dominance over one's rivals was sought as much for spiritual or emotional reasons as for material gain.

Within certain cultures, war had become so embedded in everyday life that no one could remember the origin of the current enmity, or even imagine existence without it. "We cannot live without war," said a Cherokee warrior. "Should we make peace with our present enemy, we must at once look out for some other people with whom we can indulge in our beloved occupation." White observers sometimes misinterpreted this as blood lust. But not even the bitterest rivals tried to annihilate their foes. As dedicated warriors, they needed their enemies and usually found ways of striking at them without causing them irreparable harm.

The influx of Europeans had a profound impact on Indian warfare. It did not radically reshape every battle; as late as the mid-19th century, the Quechan and Maricopa and their respective allies could fight with the old weapons and for the old reasons. But the gun, the horse, and other enticing commodities introduced to the New World by the white man altered both the way and the why of Indian fighting. Early on, many eastern tribes found that they could obtain such prizes only by allying themselves militarily with the Dutch, French, or English. A few native groups grew stronger in the process by amassing guns and other assets, but their gain was another tribe's loss as intertribal conflict grew fiercer and deadlier.

The destabilizing effect of European policies and weaponry was exemplified by the fortunes of the Iroquois League—a confederacy of five tribes occupying much of what is now upstate New York. The league, instituted before whites first reached the area in the 16th century, was formed largely to put a stop to the bitter blood feuds that had raged among the five tribes. Confederation enabled the Iroquois to present a united front against outside rivals such as the Huron and Algonquian of southern Canada, who were profiting by close trading ties with French colonists. Seeing an opportunity to thwart the French, the Dutch and later the English formed pacts with the Iroquois and plied them with firearms in exchange for furs. Dutch-supplied guns helped the Iroquois overrun the Huron in 1649 and deal a setback to the French in the process. But the Iroquois did not stop there. Over the next several decades, they ran roughshod over tribes to their north, west, and south. Expeditions of 1,000 or more Iroquois swept through the Ohio Valley as far as the Mississippi River. Tribes displaced by this onslaught then had to contend with others for resources and territory.

Other effects of the European presence on Indian warfare were no less dramatic and debilitating. By paying bounties for the scalps of their native and white enemies, for example, the colonists so encouraged scalping by Indian warriors that some chroniclers later mistakenly concluded that Europeans had instituted the practice. Although no one knows with certainty when scalping began in North America, the custom was well established by the time the first white men reached the continent. As early as 1535, the French explorer Jacques Cartier saw the results of it on his second voyage up the Saint Lawrence River when he reported that Indians displayed to him the "skins of five men's heads, stretched on hoops, like parchment." Five years later, on the Florida peninsula, the members of Hernando de Soto's pioneering Spanish expedition experienced the practice firsthand when one of their number was killed and scalped by Apalachee Indians.

Scalping appalled many Europeans, although barbarities such as beheading, disemboweling, and drawing and quartering were common enough back home. In many parts of the world, in fact, warriors were given to claiming as trophies the bodily appendages of slain enemies—

including heads, fingers, or ears. In North America, scalp taking may have evolved from headhunting, and certain tribes remained satisfied with the original. Groups such as the Kwakiutl on the Northwest Coast brought home the heads of their enemies and decorated them with bird's down. Other tribes such as the Creek of the Southeast claimed an arm or a leg instead. But scalp taking—which typically entailed removing a patch of skin approximately six inches in diameter from the crown of the skull—enjoyed wide appeal, in part because, unlike a head or an arm, a scalp could be preserved indefinitely.

For some tribes, an enemy scalp was not merely a reward for fighting but a compelling reason for doing battle in the first place. Native Americans believed that the patch of skin on top of the head and the hair that grew there represented the warrior's living spirit. To symbolize this, a warrior might wear his hair in a single lock, or scalp lock, which he usually braided and decorated with feathers and other ornaments that marked his achievements and honors. For another warrior to touch the scalp lock was an insult. Even though a man might survive a scalping, he became an outcast in the eyes of his peers.

Certain tribes on the Great Plains such as the Sioux initiated scalp raids against the enemy in order to replace the lost spiritual essence of a member who had recently been killed. Bringing home the enemy scalp was intended to alleviate the grief of survivors, which was often so intense that widows thrashed about or even gashed themselves with knives. Some women used the hair of the scalp to dry their tears.

Although Europeans did not introduce the practice of scalping, they provided it with impetus when they put a price on the scalps of their enemies, thus transforming what formerly had been a ritual act with spiritual roots into a commercial transaction. Scalping became an industry, fostered initially by the Dutch in New York in the mid-17th century and later by the French and the English. The market in enemy scalps boomed, and within a century, the colony of Pennsylvania was offering a bounty equal to $134 for an adult male scalp taken from a hostile party. Under the English bounty system, scalp takers seeking a reward could no longer keep the trophy for ritual purposes but had to surrender it to officials. Scalps redeemed for a bounty were burned or buried, except in Salem in colonial Massachusetts; there, they were displayed on the walls of the town courthouse as brazenly as in any Indian village.

The bounty system presented practical as well as ethical problems for the authorities. English colonial officials endeavored to determine the

Believed to contain a person's soul, a scalp claimed by a Crow warrior in the early 1800s is stretched over a wooden hoop and kept for ceremonial purposes.

best means of distinguishing a French scalp from one of their own. They also debated the proper minimum age of a victim to which the bounty applied—10, 15, or 16 years. The authorities had to be on the lookout for fraud and subterfuge, too. Cherokees who were in the service of the English on the Pennsylvania and Virginia frontiers in 1757, for example, proved adept at multiplying their bounties by subdividing the scalps they had taken. In one instance, their sleight of hand with a scalping knife appeared to transform five French victims into 20.

Paying for an act that they condemned as barbarous may have troubled the consciences of some colonists, but such misgivings failed to put a stop to scalp bounties. Ministers promoted scalping expeditions from the pulpits of their churches. Anglo-American woodsmen bearing fresh scalps strutted down the streets of Boston, Albany, and other colonial towns. Souvenir scalps even proved to be popular conversation pieces in the fashionable parlors back in London. A British general, George Townshend, took home such a souvenir, along with some scalping knives and a living memento of the New World—an 11-year-old Indian boy. Townshend, who gave the youngster as a servant to a nobleman, Lord George Sackville, noted that Lord Sackville nearly came to grief during a visit to the general's home, where the boy found a box containing a "scalp which he knew by the hair belonged to one of his own nation. He grew into a sudden fury and catching up one of the scalping knives made at his master

Performing the Scalp Dance, Hidatsa women of the upper Missouri region honor warriors of the tribe by displaying enemy scalps on long poles in this 19th-century depiction by Karl Bodmer. Such dances were usually performed to recall valiant war deeds and commemorate the transfer of spiritual power from vanquished to victor.

with intention to murder him." Lord Sackville managed with some difficulty to pacify the boy, but the incident served as a reminder that the violence the Europeans were promoting could come back to haunt them.

Even when the bounty system was at its height, Indian warriors commonly sought other rewards besides scalps. Prominent among the incentives that drew men into battle was the chance to claim captives. Some tribes, including the Iroquois, tortured male prisoners to death in retribution for similar deeds by the enemy. But such captives might also be kept alive and adopted by members of the victorious tribe as substitutes for dead husbands, brothers, or sons—a practice that increased in frequency as strife and European-borne diseases depleted tribal ranks. The Iroquois crowned their crushing defeat of the rival Huron, for example, by adopting entire Huron villages. In many parts of the continent, captured women were taken as wives by triumphant warriors. Alternatively, captives of either sex might be kept as slaves; the Natchez Indians of the Southeast mutilated male prisoners by cutting the tendons of their feet so that they could not escape bondage.

Along the Northwest Coast, some tribes regularly attacked their rivals for the purpose of taking slaves. Ostensibly, such raids might be mounted to avenge a past insult on the part of the enemy and restore the tribe's honor, but the ulterior motive was to capture booty, notably the human variety. The attackers swept down by night on unsuspecting villages in big war canoes and made off with food, furs, and any number of men, women, and children to replenish their supply of slaves, who typically composed between 10 and 30 percent of the tribe's population. These captives performed a great deal of the tedious labor that was required to sustain the community, such as drying fish and stretching furs. After European ships began visiting the Northwest Coast region in the late 18th century to trade for sea otter skins and other pelts, the coastal tribes discovered a new and lucrative use for female slaves: They offered their favors to crewmen for payment.

The mere ownership of slaves was a mark of social prestige in the Northwest. Many tribal chiefs possessed a dozen or more slaves each. On occasion, they might distribute some of them to subordinates along with other gifts at the lavish feasts known as potlatches, during which the host defined his social standing through the presents he doled out. War captives were also exchanged in the thriving slave trade that grew up along

A Scene on the FRONTIERS as Practiced by the HUMANE BRITISH and their WORTHY ALLIES.

Bring me the Scalps and the King our master will reward you.—

Reward for Sixteen Scalps

*Arise Columbia's Sons and forward press,
Your Country's wrongs call loudly for redress;
The Savage Indian with his Scalping knife,
Or Tomahawk may seek to take your life,*

*By bravery aw'd they'll in a dreadful Fright,
Shrink back for Refuge to the Woods in Flight;
Their British leaders then will quickly shake,
And for those wrongs shall restitution make.*

An anti-British propaganda cartoon of the Revolutionary War period depicts an Indian handing over a scalp to a British agent while another Indian scalps a Yankee settler. As it happened, both British and Yankee officials granted bounties to Indians for the scalps of those on the opposing side.

the coast, with a single able-bodied captive fetching up to 100 blankets. Along the Columbia River, a slave market emerged at The Dalles, a 15-mile stretch of rapids where traders from the interior met with their counterparts from the coast. There and elsewhere by the 19th century, warriors could swap captives for the European guns and ammunition needed for further profitable raids against their neighbors.

Apart from such forays for slaves and other prizes, the tribes of the Northwest Coast generally avoided large-scale combat, perhaps because they found trade and other forms of bloodless competition more rewarding. Several groups in the area engaged in symbolic alternatives to all-out warfare. The Tlingit of southern Alaska sometimes conducted sham battles in which they only appeared to fight vigorously with lances and daggers. Tribes of Puget Sound and areas to the south frequently settled disputes that arose between villages with abbreviated combat followed by

lengthy peace negotiations culminating in paid compensation for every death, injury, or property loss caused by either side. Even the potlatch, with its exchanges of food, property, and slaves, sometimes helped defuse potential conflicts between neighbors. Among the Kwakiutl, in fact, the potlatch evolved into a kind of substitute for battle, with warriors approaching a feast in a stealthy manner as if they were about to pounce on an enemy, only to be soothed by a generous gift from their host.

While the warriors of the Northwest Coast specialized in human booty, their counterparts on the Plains coveted plunder of the four-footed variety. Among the preeminent raiders of livestock were the Apache, an Athapaskan-speaking people who had filtered down from Canada into the southwestern grasslands by the time Europeans reached the area. For some bands, marauding for livestock and other sustenance was not a diversion but a means of subsistence. The Western Apache, for example, raised only about 25 percent of their food; the rest had to be hunted, gathered, or stolen. Raiding was seen as a man's rightful task, and anyone

A Klallam war party paddles past Fort Victoria, British Columbia, as warriors in the bows of the two canoes brandish the heads of slain foes as a signal of victory to onlookers watching from the shore. The severed heads, like the scalps taken by other tribes, embodied the captured spirit of the enemy.

A four-foot-tall Tlingit prow ornament once adorned an impressive war canoe. Representing an owl spirit, the carving was a powerful symbol of the owner's clan, which traced its lineage back to that spirit.

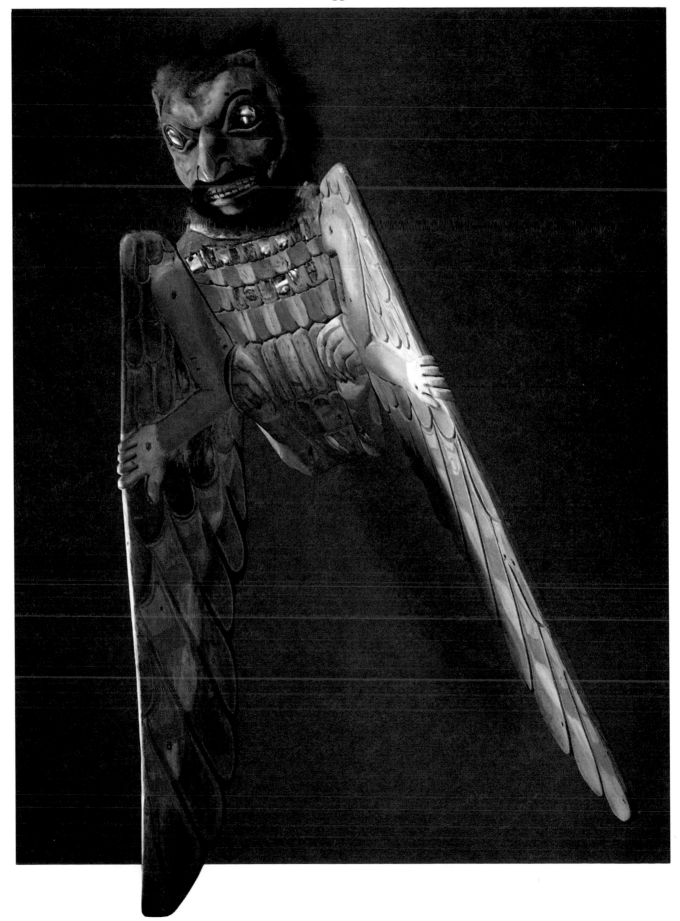

Photographed about 1903 in British Columbia, Nishga Tsimshian chiefs and members of their clan gather for a potlatch, a gift-giving ceremony that evolved into a substitute for battle among some northwestern tribes. One Kwakiutl noted in 1895: "The time of fighting has passed. We do not fight now with weapons. We fight with property."

who shirked the duty was criticized as much for laziness as for cowardice. Most men needed no coaxing and devoted themselves tirelessly to bringing home booty. It was estimated that during a four-year period in the 19th century, the Apache and their Athapaskan cousins the Navajo stole more than 450,000 sheep from Hispanic ranchers in the Southwest.

The Apache first gained notoriety as raiders in the 1500s when they began to prey on the settled Pueblo Indians. At the time, the Apache had no mounts and carried out their forays on foot. By the middle of the 17th century, the Apache were well acquainted with the horse—an animal recently reintroduced to the New World by the Spanish conquistadors, thousands of years after it became extinct in America. The horse revolutionized Apache raiding parties. The mounts themselves became prized objects of plunder, along with sheep and other livestock brought by the Spaniards. Raiders could now ride horses to steal other horses, although they usually dismounted when they neared their objective and sneaked up on foot. If they could make off with the animals undetected, so much the better, but they were prepared to fight anyone who tried to stop them or pursued them back to their villages.

Over the years, mounted Apaches ranged ever farther afield in pursuit of fresh herds. By the 19th century, they were marauding down into northern Mexico so frequently that one Apache said, "It was almost as if I had grown up there." The raiders would operate in the regions of Sonora and Chihuahua for up to 80 days at a stretch, and every mountain and town came to have an Apache name along with a Spanish one. Usually armed with traditional weapons such as bows and arrows, spears, knives, and clubs rather than firearms, the Apache were careful not to drive away the Mexican ranchers or take their land. They regarded the ranches as renewable resources and took only what they needed, leaving enough behind for the Mexicans to rebuild the herds for later Apache culling.

Even after acquiring firearms, warriors carried shields such as this Apache model from the 1880s for spiritual protection. The rawhide disk could not deflect bullets, but depictions of thunder and lightning and the thunderbird on the shield's cover were thought to keep danger away.

Still, bloody vendettas developed between the raiders and the Mexicans they pillaged, and Apache youths were raised to do battle with the ranchers as well as steal from them. For boys who were aspiring to manhood, the hope of claiming horses or other material prizes was secondary to the desire to prove through acts of bravery that they were worthy of full membership within the family and tribe. They learned courage and daring through the rough games they played with other boys, through stirring communal rituals of song and dance that celebrated feats of war, and through lessons instilled in them by their mothers, sisters, and sweethearts, who cherished bravery in a man above all else.

A Western Apache warrior named Palmer Valor who came of age in the mid-19th century recalled that his mother had encouraged him to swim in icy streams and endure other hardships when he was a boy so that he would be ready to take on any opponent. "If Mexicans or other enemies should come here," she told him, "you will get scared and be no good if you don't make yourself brave by swimming in the cold water." So intent was he on demonstrating his fortitude that he joined his first raid into Mexico when he was still a youngster. "What's the matter, little boy?" the men in the party chided him. "We are going a long way, and we will be gone for 59 days. You are too small to go with us." Yet he refused to be put off and remained with the raiders to learn from their example. The expedition he took part in had mixed results. The Apache corralled a herd of horses below the border, but two of their best men were killed when an angry band of Mexicans ambushed them.

For the Western Apache, the loss of even a few men to the enemy was a serious matter. After the raiders returned to their village, leaders called a council to consider the appropriate response. "Some horses were butchered to feed the people," Valor recalled, "and they put up a dance which lasted for about two nights. Right after the dance was finished, about two hundred of us men started off on the warpath to Mexico. They said that we were going to kill every Mexican that we met." In contrast to the typical livestock raid, when the Apache did all they could to avoid detection, this war party sought out the enemy to exact retribution. According to Valor, he and his fellow warriors killed 20 Mexicans and brought back a single captive, who was forced to take part in an Apache victory dance. "The next morning," he recollected, "an old woman there took up a spear and ran at the Mexican and stuck it right through him and killed him. This old woman was the sister of one of the two men who had been killed by the Mexicans, and this man, her brother, had been a chief. That's the way they did—one night they danced with the Mexican, and the next morning they killed him. Now the dance was finished."

An Apache scout sits proudly atop his horse. When Spanish invaders introduced horses to the Southwest during the early 1600s, the animal changed both the methods and motives of warfare for the Apache.

The Mexicans became so frustrated by Apache predations that the Sonoran government instituted a $100 bounty for the scalp of an adult male Apache. Several bounty hunters reportedly collected up to $40,000 for the scalps they took, but Apache hunting was a perilous enterprise. Taking a warrior's scalp brought prompt reprisals in the form of large Apache war expeditions. The war aims of the Apache eventually transcended revenge for the killing of individuals and became a matter of collective survival. Among the first to challenge the Spanish invaders during the 16th century, they were the last to give up the struggle against the U.S. Cavalry some 300 years later. Leaders such as Cochise and Geronimo ranked among the most revered of Indian warriors. The respect they commanded from their people was a reflection of their spiritual authority no less than their physical prowess. It was said that one night, when a detachment of cavalrymen had camped within striking distance of Geronimo and his followers, the great chief prevailed on the spirits to delay the sunrise, enabling the Apaches to slip quietly away while the soldiers slept.

General George Crook, the U.S. Army commander who finally subdued Geronimo and his warriors in the 1880s, extolled the Apache as "tigers of the human species," although the Apache themselves attributed their daunting reputation in battle as much to shrewdness as to ferocity. As Palmer Valor put it succinctly, a man who hoped to survive on the warpath "had to be mean and smart."

The Apache fought at the southern periphery of the arena of conflict dominated by the enduring emblem of Indian bravery—the horse-

An Indian Horse Dance.

Four riders and their highly trained mounts are shown performing the Horse Dance in this painting by Kills Two, an Oglala Sioux artist. The horses and riders are painted to represent a storm and wear emblems linking them to the power of the buffalo, including the horns on the three rear horses and the leggings and masks on the front rider and mount; the animal's headgear is similar to the Sioux mask at right, made for a horse. Among some Indian tribes, the dance evolved into a preparation for war.

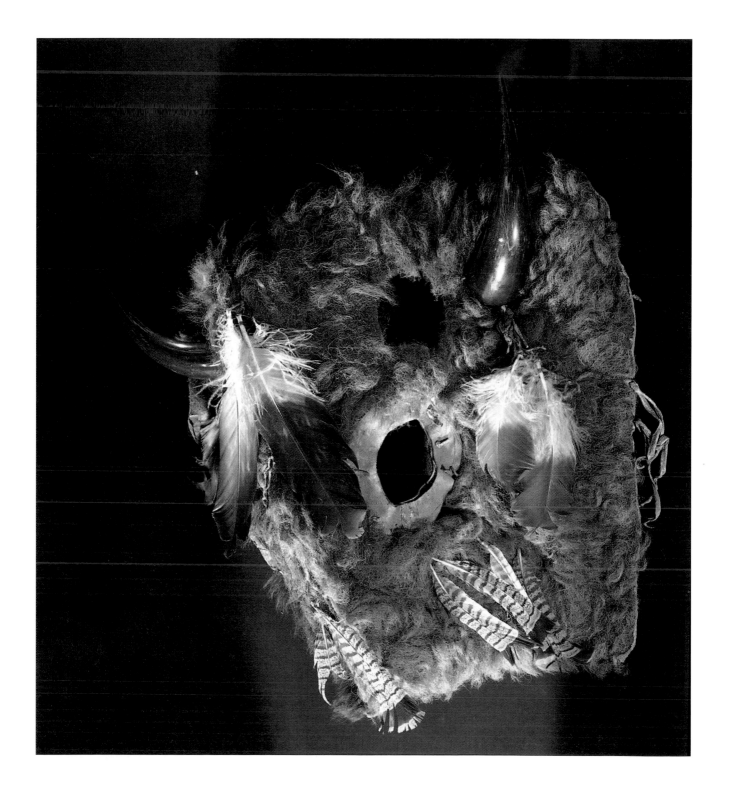

mounted warrior. Dozens of hard-riding tribes inhabited the Great Plains, which stretched from Texas northward into Canada and from west of the Mississippi to the eastern slopes of the Rockies. On this sweeping stage unfolded a panorama of chronic discord and conspicuous daring.

Once introduced to the region, the horse became both the means and the end of conflict there. Funneling up out of Mexico mostly through Apache hands, stolen or stray horses with Spanish brands reached the northern Plains around 1700 and began transforming the ways in which people lived and fought. No longer forced to hunt on foot, mounted parties could now pursue the migrating herds of bison far beyond the old hunting grounds, using draft horses in place of dogs to haul their tipis and other possessions. Around the same time, the hunters of the Plains acquired firearms, which increased their take significantly. Buffalo meat became so abundant that many tribes began to worry less about subsistence and devote more time to warlike pursuits—in particular, raids that brought the tribe additional horses, which figured prominently in social transactions such as courtship. Among the Blackfeet of the northern Plains, the so-called bride price paid by a prospective groom to a father for his daughter's hand in marriage was typically quoted in numbers of horses. It was said that a young suitor had to participate in at least a half-dozen horse raids before corralling enough animals to fulfill the bride price; a warrior who could meet that standard was considered worthy for his generosity no less than his courage.

For such personal reasons as well as for practical ones, no tribe could get enough horses. A family of six might employ up to twice that many mounts: several as beasts of burden, one horse for each member to ride on the trail, a speedy mount for chasing down bison, and a war-horse. Every tribe raided enemies to bolster its own herds. By the 19th century, probably 100 times as many horses were being stolen on the Plains as were being obtained through legitimate trade. The Crow Indians along the Yellowstone River became particularly rich in horseflesh. One year, according to a Crow chief, his tribe stole 5,000 horses from the Comanche and another 3,500 from the Kutenai and the Cheyenne combined. At the same time, he said, the Crow lost 3,000 to their northern neighbors, the Blackfeet, but struck back by taking 7,000 from those people.

From their base near the Canadian border, the powerful Blackfeet reached out in every direction for horses. They ranged through the treacherous passes of the Rockies and as far south as the Rio Grande, well over 1,000 miles from home. "Except during the bitterest weather of

SKETCHES FROM A WARRIOR'S PAST

The warrior named Medicine Crow grew up fast. Born into the Crow Indian tribe in 1848, he became acquainted with war as a mere boy, and by the age of 22, he had earned the status of chief through his exploits on the battlefield. And as he grew older, he continued to amass battle honors in the nearly incessant struggles with traditional enemies, the Sioux, the Snake, and the Blackfeet. As his fighting days dwindled, this distinguished warrior *(shown left at age 32)* was encouraged by Charles Barstow, a clerk at the Crow Agency, to preserve the memory of his valorous deeds on paper. Around 1880, he took up pencil and ink and began to make a pictorial record that would range from his first encounter with the enemy in 1864 *(shown below)* to his successes at the Battle of the Rosebud 12 years later, where he joined with the U.S. Cavalry against the Sioux.

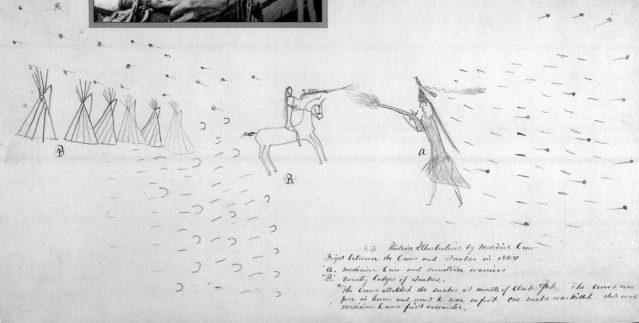

Using solitary figures to symbolize war parties, Medicine Crow depicted an encounter with mounted Snake warriors near their camp, drawing himself with long red hair and his signature—the raven or crow—perched on his head. Barstow wrote the explanatory notes.

In the two encounters shown above, Medicine Crow, identified by the raven, confronts his enemies barehanded. During the battle this drawing represents, Medicine Crow killed a Sioux warrior and later presented the dead man's scalp to his artistic mentor, Barstow.

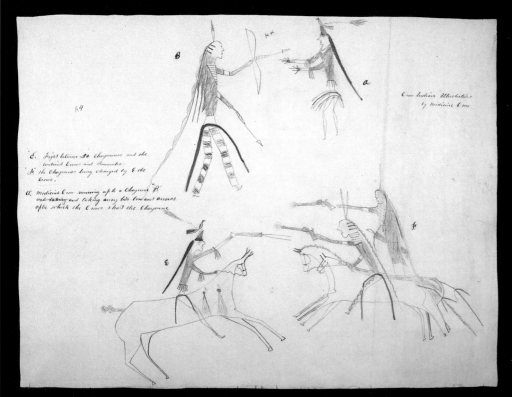

In the top drawing at left, Medicine Crow (right) prepares to count coup by wresting a bow and arrow from the hands of his Cheyenne adversary, one of the four tasks required to attain the status of chief. Below, he continues to fight against the odds despite a wound to his horse.

Leaving the Battle of the Rosebud site in the company of a flag-bearing soldier, Medicine Crow flaunts four Sioux scalps and leads a horse that, from the heavy hoofprints, symbolizes many captured animals. The enemy dead are depicted by the single body lying near the enemy camp.

Above, Medicine Crow withdraws hastily from a Sioux camp on the Yellowstone River after snatching two picketed horses and a mule. An act of such daring was esteemed by the Crow, who shared the penchant of other Plains peoples for horse raiding.

the winter," an observer wrote in the 19th century, "war parties of Black-feet were constantly out, searching for camps of their enemies, from whom they might capture horses." Someone counted more than 20 raids in one year, many of them against the Crow, who were known to have some of the best mounts on the northern Plains. Such forays by the Blackfeet and other tribes stirred up fresh enmities and revived old ones.

The introduction of the horse was not the only cause of increased conflict on the Plains. Another was the influx of tribes that began in the late 17th century as the European impact on eastern tribes triggered a chain reaction of clashes and displacements. By 1650 Cree Indians well stocked with French firearms were ranging southward from Canada into present-day Minnesota, near the Mississippi River headwaters, where they harried the tribe known to them as the Sioux, or "snake." Intimidated by enemy firepower and lured by the buffalo that carpeted the plains to the west, bands of Sioux left their homeland and moved toward the Missouri River. By 1750 they had acquired both the gun and the horse and were flexing their newfound muscle. They hunted buffalo and mounted war expeditions against competing bands, uprooting settled tribes much as they themselves had been ousted by the Cree. The western branch of the Sioux, known as the Lakota, fostered some of the great war chiefs of the Plains, including the legendary Sitting Bull.

As with the Sioux, the rigors of exile made other displaced tribes tougher and more formidable in combat. Around 1700, for unknown reasons, the people who became known as the Comanche split off from their fellow Shoshone in the northwestern plateau and migrated southward. The Comanche had already acquired some horses and soon amassed more as they clashed with various tribes along the way. So skilled did they become at mounted plunder and predation, they intimidated even the Apache, driving them westward from the vicinity of present-day Oklahoma and Texas into New Mexico and Arizona. Once ensconced in the southern Plains, the Comanche challenged all comers and ranged hundreds of miles on horseback to raid corrals and villages or to hunt bison.

Whether a tribe set out to steal horses or stalk buffalo, its warriors often found themselves tangling with human adversaries. The uneven distribution and unpredictable seasonal movements of buffalo herds inevitably brought competing bands of armed Indians into galling proximity. "We were hunting the same herds in the same place," one Sioux leg-

Led by their chief, Little Plume, a band of Blackfeet dressed for war rides across the northwestern Plains in this photograph taken around 1900 by Walter McClintock. The latter described the Blackfeet as "excellent horsemen, riding fearlessly the wildest broncos, using no saddle, and, for a bridle, only a rope passed through the horse's mouth."

end says of the strife on the Plains, "and naturally we fought." Cheyenne lore tells of an early battle that resulted when members of that tribe and the rival Assiniboin tried to surround the same buffalo herd. The Assiniboins attacked their competitors with guns, which the Cheyennes had yet to acquire. "The noise and effect of these strange weapons frightened the Cheyennes," the story goes, "and they ran away. The Assiniboins killed some of them and cut off their hair; that is, scalped them." Afterward, the Cheyennes were in shock, until a warrior rallied them with strong words. "Now we have fought with these people," he said. "They attacked us and have killed some of us. After this, let us fight with all people we meet, and we shall become great men." Like the Sioux and the Comanche, the Cheyenne responded to adversity by striving for dominance, amassing guns and horses, and inculcating in their young men a longing for battle.

Whatever factors set the stage for strife on the Plains—tribal migrations, competition for buffalo, or contention for horses—warfare became a part of the culture there to an extent unsurpassed elsewhere on the continent. Through their customs and rituals, Plains tribes perpetuated a warrior ethic that exalted combativeness and daring above all other virtues. From infancy, males in most societies were exposed to the message conveyed in the prayer that attended the birth of every Blackfeet boy. The father held the infant up to the sun and prayed, "Oh, Sun! Make this boy strong and brave. May he die in battle rather than from old age or sickness." By the time the boy reached adolescence, he knew that the route to manhood lay down the warpath. Until he had proved himself as a fighter, he could not get married or speak in council. "When we were young," recalled a 19th-century Sioux warrior named Encouraging Bear, "all we thought about was going to war."

Here, as among the Apache, girls and women played an important part in promoting bravery on the part of males. "A man could not even court a girl unless he had proved his courage," a Cheyenne warrior recalled. "A girl's mother was with her all the time, and if he walked up to her, the mother would talk about him and ask what he had done in battle." Cheyenne women would greet men who had shown weakness on the battlefield with a mocking chant: "If you had fought bravely," they gibed, "I would have sung for you." For many men, the dread of hearing such taunts was greater than their fear of death. "It was hard to go into a fight," an old warrior said, "but it was worse to turn back and face the women." A young Cheyenne who had decided to go off with a war party might sing what he called a "wolf song," telling his sweetheart of his plan. "The people all gathered to listen," another brave recalled, "and when the girl heard this, she was glad and proud. After that he did not dare to change his mind or back out of what he had decided to do."

Battle offered a young man a chance not only to win the consent of his loved one and her parents but also to literally make a name for himself. A man who endured trials on the warpath might cast off his given name and take a new one that spoke of his exploits. Sioux legend tells of such a chief who was wounded by enemy bowmen during a raid one winter and nearly died where he fell. "Lying in the snow in great pain, he hardly had the strength to sing his death song," the tale relates. "He was all alone, with neither friend nor enemy in sight." In his delirium, the chief saw two coyotes approach and heard them speak to him. "We know you!" they said, and then they lay down one on either side to warm him

A ceremonial Sioux coup stick bears the carved image of a Crow Indian, a traditional enemy of the Sioux. The owner of this stick would carry it on special occasions to show that he had counted coup.

A 1912 drawing by Lakota artist John Thunder Bear depicts the lance bearer of the Oglala Sioux Society of Braves, a fraternity of warriors, counting coup on a Crow enemy with the tip of a crooked lance.

through the night. "They licked the blood off his face. They brought him deer meat to make him strong and a sacred wound medicine." Thus fortified, the chief soon revived. "When he was able to walk, a crow came flying and guided him home. All the people marveled on seeing him and hearing his story." In tribute to the animal spirits that had come to his aid, the chief took the name Crow Coyote. Similarly, warriors from many tribes won titles that told of what they had accomplished in battle or of visions that had given them the power to overcome death and defeat.

So deeply embedded was the warrior ethic in the hearts and minds of Plains men that they came to care more for the competitive challenge of combat than for the booty they could acquire or any physical harm they could do to their enemies. To be sure, warriors might be honored for killing and scalping a foe or for capturing horses or weapons. But the exploit prized above all others was the act of touching one's opponent with a hand, stick, or weapon without drawing blood. This deed was known as counting coup, from the French word for "blow," although a soft touch was preferred over a sharp blow because it indicated scorn for the target. To count coup was to capture the spirit of the enemy.

Plains Indians extolled the feat because of the daring required to

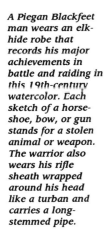

A Piegan Blackfeet man wears an elk-hide robe that records his major achievements in battle and raiding in this 19th-century watercolor. Each sketch of a horse-shoe, bow, or gun stands for a stolen animal or weapon. The warrior also wears his rifle sheath wrapped around his head like a turban and carries a long-stemmed pipe.

draw close enough on foot or on horseback to touch one's opponent. Such a foray against an armed foe required considerably more courage than targeting him at a distance with a gun or a bow. So important was counting coup to the Sioux, Crow, Arapaho, and other groups that they sometimes forsook their weapons and went into battle armed only with a wooden implement designed for touching the enemy. Called a coup stick, it ranged in length from one foot or so to 10 times that size; most were bound with animal skin or fur and decorated with feathers. Cheyenne warriors carried a stick that was striped with fur like a barber pole and proclaimed each coup by yelling, "Aaa-hey!"

In time, the term *coup* came to be loosely defined to cover other feats of bravery, which were ranked according to varying tribal conceptions of valor. The Sioux and Cree honored bringing home a scalp because it constituted proof of killing an enemy; others scorned it because lifting the scalp of a corpse entailed no particular risk. The Cree valued shooting an opponent from an exposed position over doing so from cover. The Blackfeet prized the act of wresting a firearm from an opponent. For the Crow, the challenge of sneaking into the enemy camp and stealing a single horse picketed outside the owner's tipi merited higher praise than making off with an entire herd. Indeed, the Crow ranked the theft of a picketed horse among the four exploits required for designation as a chief, or distinguished warrior. The other three were snatching away a bow or gun in a hand-to-hand encounter, leading a successful war party, and the essential coup of touching a live enemy. Along with the title of chief, the warrior might acquire a new name. One Crow chief was credited with touching seven opponents in battle and earned the name Plenty Coups.

In some tribes, women were eligible for war honors. According to Sioux legend, a young beauty called Brave Woman swore not to marry until she had avenged her dead brothers by counting coup on the Crow. She succeeded, using her father's old coup stick, but the warrior who loved her died on the same battlefield, and she spent her remaining years in mourning. A Mandan woman was credited with a coup for delivering a deadly blow. When Assiniboins attacked her village, she concealed herself by the entrance to her lodge, smashed an invader over the head with a stone mallet, and proceeded to scalp him.

Counting coup was an intricate game with complex rules. Tribal codes differed on how many warriors could be credited with a coup against the same opponent, for example. The Comanche acknowledged only the first two claims, while the Cheyenne allowed three and the Crow four—with each successive coup receiving fewer honors. Some tribes granted one warrior three coups if he first touched the enemy and then proceeded to kill and scalp him. Others acknowledged as coups daring acts that involved no contact with the foe, such as touching an enemy tipi or leaping over a fallen opponent on a horse.

However defined, a coup was rarely claimed by a warrior unless he had actually scored it. He could usually back up his assertion with the testimony of witnesses or by producing a scalp or other battlefield trophy. A notable breach of this honor code occurred when a Cheyenne brave insisted he had counted coup on a celebrated Pawnee chief named Big Eagle by the unusual stratagem of thrusting a lance through his buttocks. This incident, which resulted in the Cheyenne hero's promotion to war chief, came up some years later at a friendly meeting between the two tribes. The Pawnee chief Big Eagle rose indignantly to deny it had ever happened. To prove his case, he dramatically threw his robe aside and invited the Cheyennes to find any scars left by the lance. There were none, and the Cheyenne who had claimed the coup became an object of contempt and derision among his people.

Every Plains tribe made provision for showing off verified exploits. A warrior might portray his acknowledged coups in paintings on the covering of his tipi and his buffalo robe. He was also authorized to wear honorary insignia of various kinds. One such distinction was the tail feather of the male golden eagle, admired for its courage and swiftness; the way in which the feather was notched, painted, or otherwise altered signified the specific war honor. Crow warriors wore wolf tails at the heels of their moccasins to show that they had counted coup on the enemy, while the Comanche signified that achievement with symbols on their war shields. Mandan men could aspire to a whole host of insignia, from painted leggings to anklets made of coyote tails.

Above all, the warrior was expected to talk about his exploits. His tribe wanted strong but not silent men, who would boast of their accomplishments. Like the honors insignia, the tale the warrior told was a way of keeping the tribe informed and inspired. At victory dances and other tribal gatherings, the veteran recounted coup by evoking his experiences, sometimes to the accompaniment of drumbeats. Although such rituals were especially important to the peoples of the Plains, all tribes that engaged in combat honored their successful warriors. In the words of proud fighting men on the Plains, to journey down the warpath in memory was to recall a time "when our hearts sang for joy." ◆

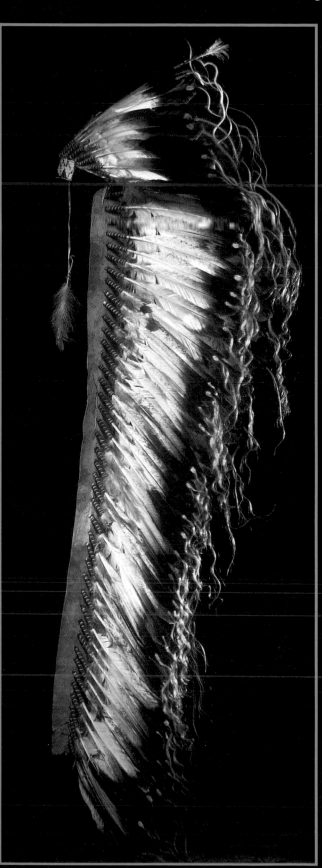

CROWNING GLORIES

In 1867 the Lakota tribal leaders chose the great warrior Sitting Bull as their war chief, giving him a war bonnet so splendid it trailed to the ground. Its eagle feathers reminded Sitting Bull that as a leader he should emulate that mightiest of birds, itself the representative of the thunderbird, master of storms. The headdress also exalted a communal spirit—each of its feathers had been contributed by a Lakota warrior to represent a personal act of bravery. Thus Sitting Bull would go into battle empowered by a crown that affirmed the collective valor of the Lakota people.

Worn by tribes across the continent during battle, and in rituals before and after the fray, headdresses could inspire bravery, recall past war honors, or invoke supernatural power over an enemy. The swept-back feathered headgear of the Lakota warriors began to surpass the horned bonnet in popularity among many Plains peoples, and by the end of the 19th century, it had become the most recognizable of all Native American regalia and an emblem of the Indian warrior. Many tribes also embraced the eastern woodlands custom of adorning the head with a crest of deer hair, known as a roach. Other headwear remained regionally isolated, such as the effigy helmets of the Northwest, carved wooden headpieces resembling those once worn by Asian fighting men. But whatever its form, the headdress was a communicator of social standing—and remained so even after tribes were confined to reservations and no longer waged war. Resplendent in feather bonnet, war cap, turban, or helmet, a man trumpeted his accomplishments in battle or his prestige within the community—in a way understood by friend and foe alike.

◀

Evoking the power of the golden eagle, this magnificent Lakota feather war bonnet was designed to sway in the breeze to bring to mind the bird of prey's wing beats.

An Apache skin skullcap from the 1880s is adorned with feathers, silver buttons, and beaded designs. A medicine bundle is attached to the side of the cap to protect the wearer in battle.

While most war bonnets displayed feathers of raptorial birds, this horned headdress features swan feathers. The headpiece was captured from its Assiniboin owner by a Crow enemy, Bear in the Water.

In traditional Blackfeet style, the feathers of this ermine-trimmed war bonnet stand almost straight up, supported by sticks wrapped in porcupine quills.

This headdress of beads, bear claws, quills, and dangling ermine was worn during ceremonies performed by the Blackfeet All Brave Dog Society. Warrior societies exerted a powerful influence on the development of such flamboyant headwear.

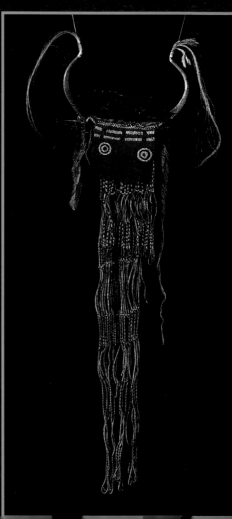

A headpiece such as this Potawatomi otter fur turban, bedecked with glass beads, indicated high social standing among men of the Plains and Great Lakes tribes.

This Apache buffalo horn headdress has a buckskin trailer fringed with the tail feathers of fledgling bald and golden eagles. Such a headpiece would have been worn by only the most prominent of warriors.

Strictly for ceremonial use, this northern Plains headdress was worn by members of the Buffalo Bulls warrior society during their Buffalo Dance.

This carved wooden Tlingit helmet, with its fearsome visage, towered above the head, giving the wearer intimidating height. The separate collar protected most of the face and neck. Between the pieces was a narrow gap for the eyes.

Worn in the hair at the back of the head, a Lakota hide headpiece decorated with porcupine quills also features trimmed eagle feathers.

Covered with blazing red and orange rooster hackles, this spectacular Plains headdress, dating from around 1890, is a product of the reservation era.

This stylized Iroquois
bonnet, with its pro-
fusion of hawk
feathers and beaded
designs, was made
in the late 1800s for
show or sale to
whites. Additional-
ly, feathered bon-
nets were worn by
Iroquois leaders at
tribal gatherings.

This Plains roach of
dyed deer hair and
trimmed feathers
was attached to the
warrior's scalp lock
for ceremonial
dances and undulat-
ed as he moved.

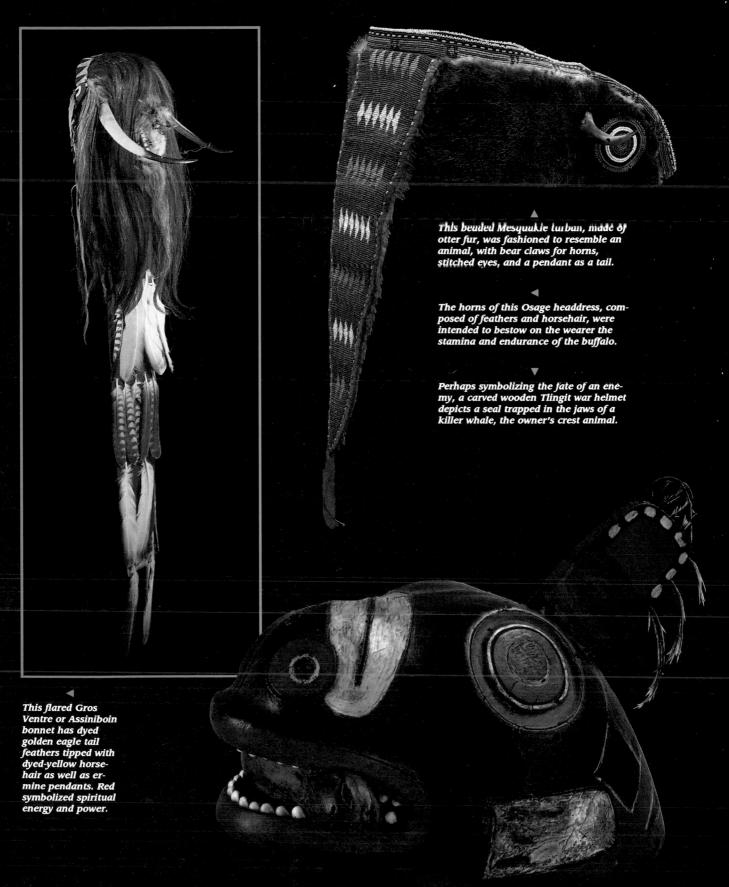

This beaded Mesquakie turban, made of otter fur, was fashioned to resemble an animal, with bear claws for horns, stitched eyes, and a pendant as a tail.

The horns of this Osage headdress, composed of feathers and horsehair, were intended to bestow on the wearer the stamina and endurance of the buffalo.

Perhaps symbolizing the fate of an enemy, a carved wooden Tlingit war helmet depicts a seal trapped in the jaws of a killer whale, the owner's crest animal.

This flared Gros Ventre or Assiniboin bonnet has dyed golden eagle tail feathers tipped with dyed-yellow horsehair as well as ermine pendants. Red symbolized spiritual energy and power.

A HERO OF THE MANDAN NATION

"Free, generous, elegant and gentlemanly in deportment—handsome, brave and valiant," wrote artist George Catlin in 1832 of the Mandan war chief Mató-Tópe, esteemed military figure of the northern Plains. Mató-Tópe's name, which means "the Four Bears," was legend among the upper Missouri tribes. He was said to have killed 14 of his enemies. Dressed for war, as in Swiss painter Karl Bodmer's 1834 watercolor *(opposite),* his entire person bore a record of battlefield exploits: stripes representing coups, hair ornaments counting the wounds he had sustained, and a handprint signifying the prisoners he had taken. Mató-Tópe's friendship with white men such as Catlin, Bodmer, and German explorer Prince Maximilian zu Wied brought him fame far beyond his homeland. But he lived to bitterly regret his generosity. In 1837 an epidemic of smallpox, a disease introduced by whites, all but wiped out the Mandan tribe. The great warrior could only watch helplessly as his wives, children, and comrades died. "I do not fear death," he declared, "but to die with my face rotten that even wolves will shrink at seeing me and say to themselves, that is the Four Bears, the friend of the whites." He then wrapped himself in his bison robe and surrendered to death.

The six painted sticks that Mató-Tópe wore in his hair each represented a musket wound received in battle. A red wooden knife recalled his best-known victory—the slaying of a Cheyenne chief in hand-to-hand combat.

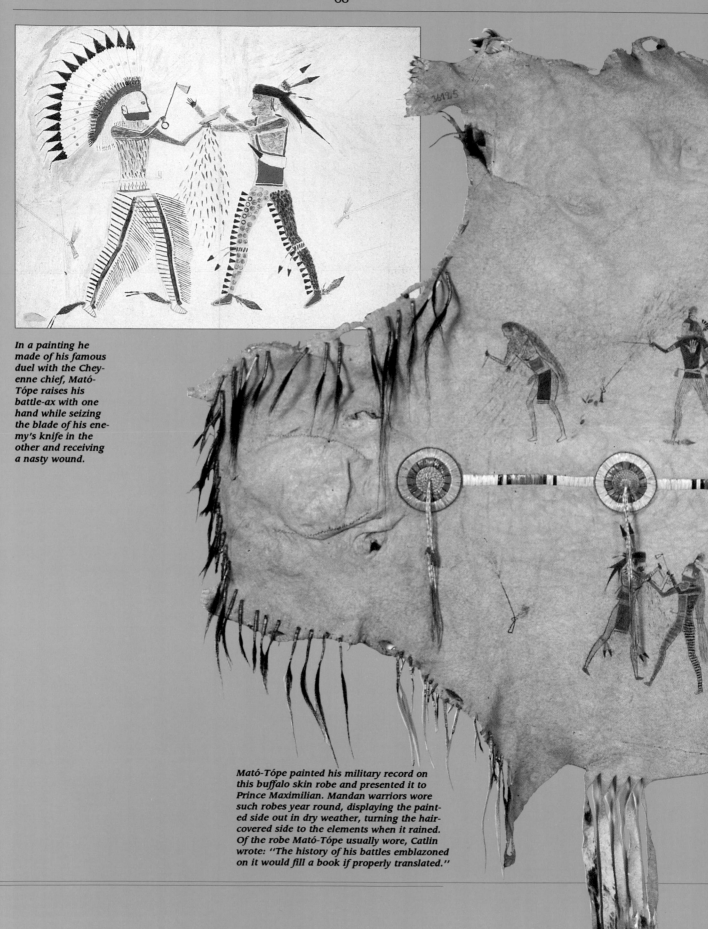

In a painting he made of his famous duel with the Cheyenne chief, Mató-Tópe raises his battle-ax with one hand while seizing the blade of his enemy's knife in the other and receiving a nasty wound.

Mató-Tópe painted his military record on this buffalo skin robe and presented it to Prince Maximilian. Mandan warriors wore such robes year round, displaying the painted side out in dry weather, turning the hair-covered side to the elements when it rained. Of the robe Mató-Tópe usually wore, Catlin wrote: "The history of his battles emblazoned on it would fill a book if properly translated."

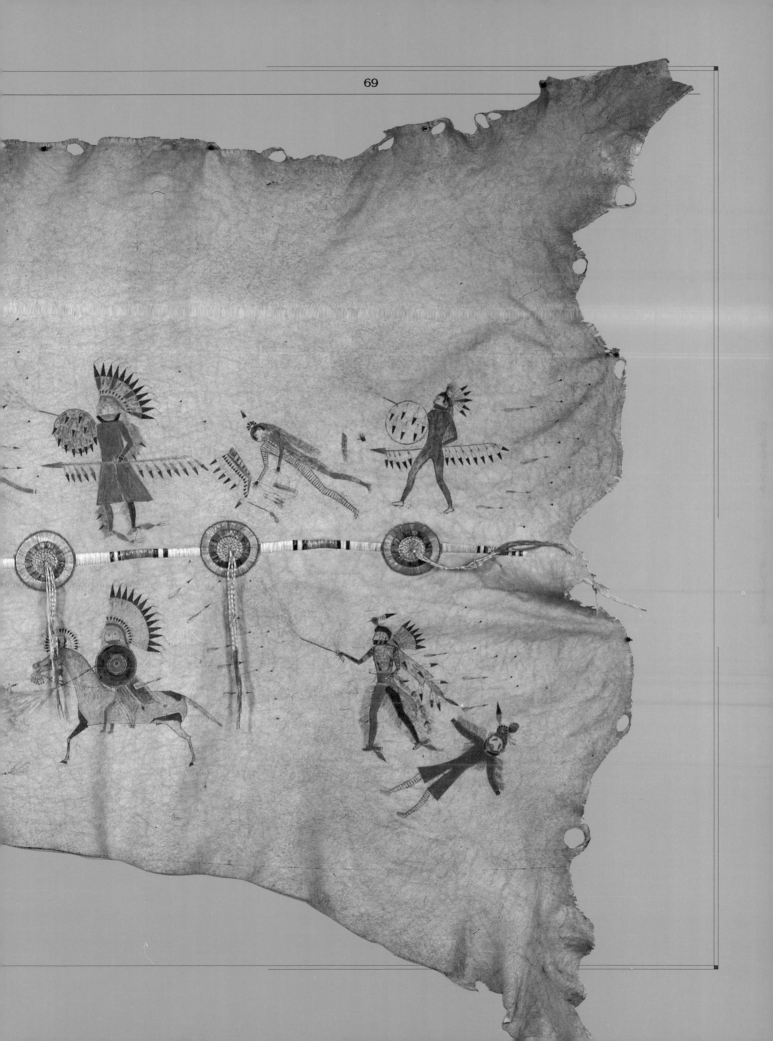

Mató-Tópe's bone war whistle was wrapped in colored porcupine quills. Warriors went into battle with whistles hung around their necks to signal one another when they came upon an enemy.

Forty eagle feathers, each representing a battlefield coup, were sewn to Mató-Tópe's ceremonial headdress, denoting the Mandan hero's elevated status.

Bear claw ornaments such as this necklace made by Mató-Tópe were potent testimony to the wearer's courage. Few men were brave enough to hunt the ferocious grizzly, respected by the Indians as the most powerful of nature's creatures.

Mató-Tópe's painted antelope skin shirt was probably worn only in the coldest weather or on ceremonial occasions. Mandan warriors customarily wore little more than paint on their upper bodies beneath their heavy bison robes.

G. Catlin.

The Author painting a Chief, at the base of the Rocky Mountains.

Mató-Tópe painted this self-portrait on paper supplied by Bodmer, depicting himself holding a feather-bedecked shield. His insignia, a pair of ceremonial lances, are shown thrust into the ground at his side.

In a sketch Catlin made of a portrait-painting session, Mató-Tópe poses for the artist surrounded by a coterie of admirers. Catlin likened his subject to a Roman gladiator, writing that the Mandan stood "with the sternness of a Brutus and the stillness of a statue."

In Bodmer's formal portrait, Mató-Tópe holds the lance that as a young warrior he pulled from the body of his slain brother. He later used the weapon to avenge his brother's death, creeping alone into the killer's camp to spear the man in his own tipi. The scalp he took that night dangles from the shaft.

2

THE RITUAL OF WARFARE

Evoking centuries of Indian warfare, the fearsome mask at left with its double topknot of fur was worn by Cherokee warriors during the elaborate rituals they performed before launching attacks on enemy tribes. Masks were also used after the fighting during the Cherokee's victory ceremonies.

By 1830 the Cheyenne and the Pawnee had been bitter adversaries for decades. Almost every summer, rival war parties crossed the Plains to steal horses, raid villages, and count coup. Sometimes the Cheyenne surprised the Pawnee; at other times the Pawnee stunned the Cheyenne. Recalling those days, some Cheyennes compared the two nations to a pair of buffalo bulls in rutting season, butting each other to exhaustion and then panting side by side until they could muster the strength to resume the fight.

But this year promised to be different. This time the Cheyenne intended to fight with a spiritual weapon more powerful than their bows and arrows, lances, or war clubs. For only the third time in tribal memory, and for the first time against the Wolf People, as they called the Pawnee, the Cheyenne were going into battle armed with their holiest medicine—the Sacred Arrows and the Sacred Buffalo Hat.

Those two Great Mysteries were gifts from the Cheyenne supreme being, Maheo. According to tradition, Maheo bestowed the Sacred Arrows on Sweet Medicine, a legendary hero of the Cheyenne, so that his people would have power over the animals as well as over the men of other tribes. The gift consisted of two Man Arrows and two Buffalo Arrows, all painted red and black. Maheo bestowed the Sacred Buffalo Hat on another Cheyenne hero, called Erect Horns. Made from the horned scalp of a female buffalo, the hat ensured the perpetuation of the herds of bison that were essential to the tribe's survival. The Cheyenne who set out against the Pawnee in the summer of 1830 firmly believed that if they observed the proper ceremonies, the two Great Mysteries would blind their foe and bring them a tremendous victory.

Led by the Arrow Keeper, White Thunder, who partook of the holiness of Sweet Medicine himself, the entire tribe broke camp. No member of the community was left behind when the Sacred Arrows traveled. Once the Cheyenne had reached Pawnee territory, in present-day Nebraska, women, children, and old men pitched their tipis in a safe location while scouts sought out the enemy. All signs remained auspicious until Chey-

enne warriors came upon the bodies of four of their scouts, whom the Pawnees had evidently caught by surprise. The sight of their slain companions inflamed the Cheyennes, and they drove their horses all night until they came within sight of a Pawnee village.

Shortly after daybreak, the lurking Cheyennes noticed a Pawnee hunting party preparing for a buffalo chase. The war chiefs ordered the assault on the village delayed until after the hunters had departed. But when several hunters rode close to the spot where the Cheyennes lay in hiding, the headstrong warriors could contain themselves no longer.

Without waiting for the Arrow Keeper to conduct the blinding ceremonies that would summon the power of the Sacred Arrows, they charged. There was no time for White Thunder to chew sweet root, the holy plant into which Sweet Medicine had transformed himself, or to spit

Chief Little Wound, a Sioux, stands before a half-circle of his tribesmen, all dressed in elaborate battle regalia, during an 1898 re-creation of a tribal war council. The decision to go to war, or even to undertake a raid on an enemy, was made in many tribes by a formal council of the bravest and most respected warriors, who in turn often sought advice from medicine men and prophets as well as from women of the tribe who were thought to be especially wise.

it first to the four directions where the Sacred People dwell, and then toward the enemy. There was no time for him to dance with the Sacred Arrows in hand, thrusting them in the direction of the enemy, or to attach them in the prescribed manner to the lance held by a warrior-priest, who was supposed to approach the enemy on one flank while another warrior, wearing the Sacred Buffalo Hat, advanced on the opposite flank. Instead of tying the Man Arrows and the Buffalo Arrows onto the lance separately, White Thunder hastily attached the entire bundle, and the warrior-priest hurried into battle behind the rest of the men. The Cheyennes would pay dearly for their rashness.

As they charged across the prairie, the Cheyennes encountered a crippled Pawnee. Following a practice common among Plains Indians with fatal afflictions, the man had chosen this day to die. He was singing his death song when the first Cheyenne warriors approached, striking him with their coup sticks as they galloped by. The warrior-priest who had been entrusted with the Sacred Arrows also charged him, but his horse shied at the last second. The crippled Pawnee managed to grab the lance from the warrior-priest's hand and jerk it free. Instantly recognizing the significance of his trophy, he shouted to his fellow warriors for help. Heeding his cries, Pawnees dashed to the scene and took the lance from the crippled man. Now it was their turn to charge the Cheyennes, brandishing the captured lance. Unnerved by the loss of their medicine, the Cheyennes fled in confusion. What had been planned as their greatest victory had become their greatest defeat.

Years afterward, a Cheyenne elder recalled the long journey back to their homeland: "The whole camp was crying all the time as it moved along, mourning the loss of the medicine arrows more than the loss of the people who had been killed." Recognizing that without the Sacred Arrows the Cheyenne could no longer exist as a people, tribal medicine men eventually consecrated four substitutes, and a few years later, White Thunder himself negotiated with the Pawnee for the release of one of the originals. A second arrow was subsequently recaptured for the Cheyenne by their Sioux allies. But the stain on tribal pride remains even today, and many Cheyennes attribute their eventual defeat by the whites to that day when the unity between the people and the sacred powers was broken.

The Cheyenne catastrophe stands as an epic example of the consequences that could befall a tribe whose war leaders failed to observe proper ritual. As with every other important facet of Native American life, warfare was inextricably connected with spirituality. Success at war, like success at hunting, fishing, or planting crops, depended on every member of the community paying careful attention to the sacred ways at every step, from the days of preparation before the raid, through the arduous journey to the enemy village, to the period of purification afterward. Warriors, women, boys, shamans—sometimes even the unfortunate enemy captives—all had specific roles to play.

Although most tribes regarded armed combat as a necessary and honorable pursuit, all made a clear distinction between the Red Road of war—as Plains Indians referred to it—and the White Road of peace. To a Native American, taking any life, even that of an animal, was a solemn act that disrupted the balance and harmony of the universe. Only careful attention to ritual could protect men from the consequences of violent deeds. Warriors risked attacks not only from the living enemy but also from the spirits of the dead, who suffered torment after being wrenched from this world by acts of malice and remained outcasts until retaliation by kinsmen eased their way into the Land of Souls.

The greatest spiritual obligation belonged to the war leader. His success depended as much on his attunement to the sacred powers as on his fighting and leadership skills. A defeat, or even the loss of a single warrior, was often attributed to the misreading of omens or, as in the case of the unfortunate Cheyenne, to neglect of the rituals. Following a defeat, a war chief might be able to salvage his reputation by leading a successful expedition, but repeated failures were a clear sign of his inability to communicate effectively with the mysterious powers; few warriors would answer such a leader's next call to battle.

A successful war chief, on the other hand, seldom found it difficult to raise a war party. Recruiting methods varied from tribe to tribe. In the northern woodlands, Ojibwa war leaders paid a personal visit to each warrior. Leaders of other tribes sent couriers to the outlying encampments of their kinsmen to spread the news of the upcoming attack. In the Southeast, war chiefs solicited volunteers at ceremonies marked by dancing, chanting, and powerful oratory. The leader announced the impending expedition by circling his winter house three times while beating a drum and singing a war song. He or an elder respected for his brave deeds then addressed the assembled warriors in a commanding voice, reciting the misdeeds of the enemy and urging the listeners to exact revenge. "Never fear the arrows of the enemy," one elder implored his audience, "and let it be seen that you are men and true warriors."

Feathers, ermine tails, and dyed horsehair decorate a ceremonial rattle belonging to the Kit Fox Society, one of several warrior groups in the Mandan tribe. Societies such as the Kit Fox played vital roles in the life of most tribes and vied with each other for the honor of being the most valiant in war.

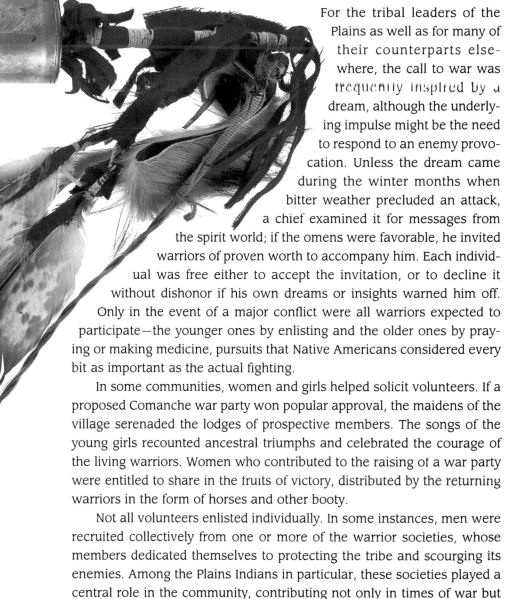

For the tribal leaders of the Plains as well as for many of their counterparts elsewhere, the call to war was frequently inspired by a dream, although the underlying impulse might be the need to respond to an enemy provocation. Unless the dream came during the winter months when bitter weather precluded an attack, a chief examined it for messages from the spirit world; if the omens were favorable, he invited warriors of proven worth to accompany him. Each individual was free either to accept the invitation, or to decline it without dishonor if his own dreams or insights warned him off. Only in the event of a major conflict were all warriors expected to participate—the younger ones by enlisting and the older ones by praying or making medicine, pursuits that Native Americans considered every bit as important as the actual fighting.

In some communities, women and girls helped solicit volunteers. If a proposed Comanche war party won popular approval, the maidens of the village serenaded the lodges of prospective members. The songs of the young girls recounted ancestral triumphs and celebrated the courage of the living warriors. Women who contributed to the raising of a war party were entitled to share in the fruits of victory, distributed by the returning warriors in the form of horses and other booty.

Not all volunteers enlisted individually. In some instances, men were recruited collectively from one or more of the warrior societies, whose members dedicated themselves to protecting the tribe and scourging its enemies. Among the Plains Indians in particular, these societies played a central role in the community, contributing not only in times of war but also in seasons of peace, when they helped regulate life in the village and maintain order on the hunt.

Warrior societies often traced their origins to heroes who communed with sacred animals or other spirits and acquired some of their power. Members of the Blackfeet Horn Society, for example, told of a man by the name of Aiakatsi, who married a female buffalo capable of assuming human form. Some time after the marriage, she returned with their son to

This war sash composed of eagle feathers strung on a red trade cloth was carried into battle by the bravest warrior of the Hidatsa tribe's Crazy Dog Society. The bearer of the sash was expected to defend it to the death.

her herd, and Aiakatsi braved numerous ordeals in the hope of winning her back from the buffalo chief. His final task was head-to-head combat with a huge buffalo bull that had laid claim to his wife. Aiakatsi prepared for the definitive battle by donning a medicine robe—the hide of a buffalo with the horns attached. According to the legend, the medicine robe transformed Aiakatsi: "He threw himself on the ground and rolled like a buffalo, and grunted. He stood up, a buffalo. He pawed the ground." With the assistance of his wife, he gored the bull to death and won her release. Wife and son took human shape, and upon their return to the Blackfeet, Aiakatsi founded the Horn Society, whose members were thought to possess such power that they could cause death without resort to a weapon.

The method of recruitment into a Plains warrior society depended on the nature of the society. In some tribes, a young man who had reached the age of a novice warrior—usually in mid-adolescence—could join any of the societies, either by invitation or by his own choice. He usually remained a member for the rest of his fighting years, which ended around the age of 40. In other tribes, however, all the young men entered a society as a group. After a few years, the entire membership passed on its ceremonies and regalia to the succeeding generation, and inherited positions in the society occupied by the next older group. This progress up the ladder of societies continued until old age brought an end to participation

Chief of the Hidatsa's Crazy Dog Society in the 1830s, a warrior named Pehriska-Ruhpa wears full ceremonial regalia in a watercolor by artist Karl Bodmer. Pehriska-Ruhpa's spiky headdress includes magpie feathers and a wild turkey tail; a war whistle and red sash hang from his neck.

in combat. Their abilities and bravery having been proved in countless battles, the retired warriors might then join a society of elders, offering their counsel and wisdom to the tribe.

Branches of the same warrior society could be found in many tribes, even among groups who regularly fought each other. One of the most prominent and prevalent warrior organizations was the Kit Fox Society, the leading group among the Sioux and an important one among several other tribes, including the Cheyenne, the Arikara, the Mandan, and the Crow. In war as well as in peace, members sought to emulate the admirable traits of the kit fox, whose skill at stalking prey was matched by its keen instinct for protecting and nurturing its own. The rules of conduct for the Sioux Kit Fox Society demanded bravery, generosity, and brotherliness; officials punished violators of the code by lashing them.

These two Indian boys wear the battle costume of warriors in the making. The Kiowa youth (left) in the beaded buckskin outfit belonged to the Rabbits, first of several war societies through which Kiowa boys progressed as they grew up. The other youngster wears the ornate striped body paint, multistrand necklace, and breechcloth that distinguished the warriors of the Southwest's Quechan tribe. In virtually all tribes, boys learned at an early age that they must become courageous fighters and that the greatest honor was to die bravely in battle.

The society's exclusive regalia included a kit fox skin worn like a poncho, head in front and tail behind. From the animal's nose hung several small medicine bags, and other parts of the pelt were adorned with porcupine quills or bells. Members also wore a broad otter skin band around the forehead, with the jawbones of several foxes, painted red or blue, fastened to the band. They attached crow feathers in a bunch to the back of the head, and stuck two upright eagle feathers in a knot of their hair. Officers of the society carried curved lances, shaped like unstrung bows and wrapped in colored sinew, cloth, and beadwork; below the lance head dangled eagle feathers. The honor of carrying such a lance brought added responsibility; the bearers were expected to stand in the front line and use the lances for counting coup.

One of the most important items in the regalia of any Plains warrior society was a decorated sash of hide or cloth, up to 12 feet in length. The sash's significance was more than symbolic. Only a man of demonstrated courage was allowed to wear it. In a pitched battle, he was expected to attach the sash to a single spot on the field and fight to the death rather than yield ground; most sashes had a slit in the end, or a special peg, to allow the attachment. In accepting the risk of wearing the sash, the warrior was simply affirming his basic obligation to seek honor at the cost of his own life, if necessary. As men of the Sioux Kit Fox Society sang before entering battle: "I am a Fox. I am supposed to die. I already threw my life away. Something daring, something dangerous, I wish to do."

Before a youngster could claim fellowship with the warriors of his tribe, he had to undergo a lengthy initiation. Almost every war party included a few teenagers aspiring to become fighting men. In most tribes, the experienced warriors limited the youths' activities to such tasks as carrying food, spare moccasins, lead ropes for captured horses, and other supplies. The boys were not considered ready for combat until they had participated in a number of raids.

Apache youngsters, for example, were required to accompany four expeditions before qualifying as full-fledged warriors. Apprenticed at puberty to the craft of war, they learned survival techniques and played at raiding games until they reached the age of 16 or so and were ready to move on to real battles. On their first outings, the boys helped with cooking and other camp chores. It was the only time in the lifetime of an Apache male when it was considered appropriate for him to perform do-

Crowds of Mandan boys fight a mock battle
outside their village in the upper Missouri
River region in a painting done around
1832 by the chronicler of Indian life George
Catlin. In fights such as these, Catlin wrote,
the boys wielded harmless wooden knives
with which they would scalp any "enemies"
they had shot with equally harmless
arrows made of reeds. Tufts of grass worn
on top of their heads served as scalps.

mestic work. The youths were obliged to speak respectfully to all the men, to avoid laughing or looking upward (which would bring down a torrential rain), and never to sleep unless granted permission. Each boy put forth his best effort, knowing that his performance under trial was regarded as prophetic of his future conduct.

The death of a novice was looked upon as a serious indictment against the leader of a raid. Usually the boys shared the hardships of the trail, but were kept out of harm's way during combat. Apprentices among the Western Apache wore a special cap decorated with hummingbird feathers so that they would move fast and not be seen by the enemy. Although they were shielded from the foe, novices were under intense scrutiny from their elders and sometimes failed their apprenticeships; leaders of future raiding parties had no interest in taking along unreliable youngsters. Those young men who passed the test, however, assumed their place among the warriors and were expected to be in the forefront of the fighting on their next outing.

The Kwakiutl of the Pacific Northwest began molding some boys for the warrior's life at birth. A father with martial ambitions for his son prepared an amulet from the tongues of a snake, lizard, and toad, and part of a grizzly bear's heart and forepaw. On the baby's fourth day, the father invoked the spirits of the animals: "The reason I took out your tongues, snake, lizard, toad, is that I want my son to be a warrior, for at the points of your tongues you keep a death bringer. Now you will give this to my son." To the bear, he said, "Let your heart give my son strength and your claws the power to strike his enemy without mercy."

Every day, parents bathed the little warrior-to-be in icy water to toughen him for his future profession. When a grizzly bear was killed, they boiled the heart to feed to him and smeared the boy's face with its blood so that he might take on the power of the animal. The final test of his suitability for the calling came when the boy was full grown: He or his father pushed the point of an awl through his forearm, so that it passed between the two bones to emerge on the other side. If the boy accepted the pain in silence, his future success in battle was ensured.

Mohave youngsters also experienced the first trials of their military mettle at an early age. A kwanami of the tribe's warrior class judged the potential of each boy when he was about five or six. The test might involve pushing the lad into a beehive, or drawing blood from his forehead with a fingernail, or lashing his back with a switch. A boy who showed stoicism or pluck was accepted as a *humar kwanami,* or half-grown war-

rior. Henceforth, while the other boys learned archery with hunting bows, he would practice with a special war bow. He ran long distances for conditioning and learned from his elders to focus his thoughts on one thing: killing the enemy. As he grew older and tougher, his mates often declined to play with him because his play had become too rough. In time, he told of the dreams that had first come to him when he was in his mother's womb and that marked him as one destined for great things in battle.

In most tribes, however, specific training for war began much later in life. Iroquois boys, for example, absorbed the lessons of warfare from an early age without special instruction. They watched the departure and return of war parties, witnessed the torture and death of prisoners, and yearned to avenge relatives lost to the enemy. A bright and ambitious child, seeing the esteem granted to the leading warriors, naturally aspired to join their ranks. Such potential warriors were left largely to their own devices. Boys roamed the woods in gangs, hunting with small bows and arrows and miniature hatchets. They competed in footraces, wrestling, and lacrosse. From time to time, male relatives tutored them in fire making, tracking, and other essential crafts. And the adults lavished praise on

In accordance with an ancient ritual, men of the Dakota Sioux prepare for a steam bath in a traditional sweat lodge—fashioned of bent saplings covered with animal hides—in a photograph that was taken in the late 1800s. The warriors of many tribes took sweat baths and performed other ritual purifications before they went into battle.

the youngsters for their first kills, interpreting them as harbingers of future *weakness. Sometimes* the youthful bands

Relic of many battles, a Sioux shield dating from the early 19th century, made of painted buffalo skin and adorned with buffalo hoofs and human scalp locks, trails an ornate tail of brass bells and eagle feathers. Such shields could deflect arrows but not bullets; still, they were prized for the spiritual protection they afforded in battle.

stayed away from the village for days at a time, living on roots, berries, and small game that they trapped or shot. As they grew older, hardier, and more skillful, the boys turned spontaneously from playing at war to the real thing.

Among the privileges a young man aspired to when he took up arms was the right to display the regalia of war—clothing and gear that were not only beautiful to behold but also charged with spiritual power. The shield of the Plains warrior, for example, was decorated with symbols derived from dreams or visions that offered the man as much protection in battle as the thick buffalo hide the images were painted on. Many warriors carried the shield in a buckskin cover to preserve its power until the fighting began. When a warrior died, his shield might be buried with him to protect him in the spirit world.

The wardrobe of a fighting man denoted his status and reputation within his community. Special headdresses and other adornments frequently signaled the presence of a war leader or other highly respected individual. Among the Comanche, who had no official warrior societies, men who wore full-feathered bonnets were recognized as war leaders. In donning the war bonnet, the leader pledged himself to live up to the highest standards of bravery. He was expected to fight fiercely, and retreat only when all the other warriors were safe; any violation of these obligations could bring public denunciation and forfeiture of the right to wear the headdress. Losing it in combat brought even greater opprobrium; thereafter, other men might impugn the manliness of the failed leader by addressing him as "elder sister."

Warriors among the Pawnee and other Plains tribes carried personal war bundles assembled with the assistance of a shaman or priest, who stipulated their contents and the ceremonies governing their use. A typical bundle might include an otter skin war collar, deerskin leggings, the specially wrapped body of a hawk, an ear of corn, and paints in black, red, yellow, and white (red, the color of war, was the most important). Some of the articles in the bundle were worn or displayed during battle to invoke spirit powers, while other items were used ritually before or after

An Ojibwa warrior's outfit includes a buckskin shirt and
leggings, a belt and sheathed
knife, and a fur headband
with long tassels. The intricate
beadwork on the leggings,
belt, and other items indicates
that the owner held a position
of high rank in the tribe.

combat. A pipe and a tobacco pouch made of the skin of a wildcat, for example, allowed the warrior to seek help from the spirits or give thanks to them by offering up sacred tobacco smoke.

Aside from such personal observances, the entire war party often joined in ceremonies before setting out from the village. Chickasaws bound for war, for example, took part in a purification rite that lasted for three days and nights. They fasted until sunset every day, while drinking freely of a purgative brew of snakeroot. Throughout the period, they were required to abstain from sex with their wives or sweethearts. The young men bore careful watching, for any violation of taboo, it was believed, would destroy the power of the purifying drink.

Among some groups, a shaman would conduct ceremonies of song and prayer in order to confirm that the war leader's plans had the blessing of the spirits. Inauspicious signs might keep the war party in camp, but if the prospects were considered favorable, the shaman himself might come along on the raid to help find or frustrate the enemy by supernatural means. Certain expeditions also included medicine men who specialized in the treatment of arrow wounds or snakebites, or in such mystic arts as locating drinking water.

Of utmost importance to the morale of men bound for battle was the War Dance—a ceremony observed by tribes all across the continent. The warriors themselves usually took the lead, but other members of the tribe often joined in to express solidarity with the fighting men. As they danced, the men sang special songs, which one Apache warrior likened to prayers. Among some tribes, if men failed to return from the expedition, people would never sing their song again.

The Ojibwa War Dance took place around the War Post, a fresh cedar pole erected in the middle of the village circle. At sunset, on the evening before the expedition was to depart, a bonfire was lighted near the pole, fueled with wood that had been collected by the youngest, untested warriors in the party, together with the other boys and girls of the village. The community was summoned to the event by the beat of a drum. The Drum Keeper proceeded to tune the instrument, using the heat of the flames. Several drummers then beat the drum together; they tapped gently at first, until they achieved a unified rhythm, then began striking harder. As the constant pulse resonated through the darkness, the lead drummer began a high-pitched chant, soon picked up by his fellows. Then, with two light taps, the lead drummer slowed the tempo. The war leader emerged from the dark, followed by his warriors, all dressed in full war regalia—

Wielding lances, guns, and clubs, Mandan warriors reach the frenzied climax of the Bison Dance in a painting by Karl Bodmer, who saw the ritual performed in 1834. Some of the dancers wear strips of buffalo hide with horns attached, others huge masks of entire buffalo heads with metal-rimmed eyeholes. The dance was performed before Mandan war parties set out on raids.

headdresses, armbands, and amulets signifying past feats. After dancing four times around the fire, brandishing clubs, and yelling a war cry, they sat down in front of the War Post.

The war leader then stood before the assembled people. As the whole village listened, the warrior chief enumerated to a recital of the grievances that required blood retribution. Pledging himself to right these wrongs, he then began to regale his followers with tales of his own military exploits. The War Dance, marking the transition from peace to war, was the only time an Ojibwa warrior might properly speak of these deeds. At the climax of each tale of combat, the leader whirled to smite the War Post with his club, symbolically smashing the enemy.

After the leader had concluded his recital by promising revenge, the second-leading warrior stood up and spoke. Rank by rank, the rest of the party made their speeches until it was the turn of the untried warriors. They had no feats of bravery to brag about, but they were permitted nonetheless to strike the War Post. The entire war party then prepared themselves for bloody deeds by eating raw liver cut from a dog that had been sacrificed before their eyes by a tribal elder.

The drumming resumed, the boys of the village stoked the fire, and the warriors followed the war chief in an increasingly frenzied dance around the flames, reenacting earlier conflicts and pouring out their emotions through song and movement. After the warriors had completed four circuits, the remainder of the tribe joined them in the dance. When the war leader sat down, the dance ended, the drum was put away, and the entire community shared in a feast.

Some tribes reserved such dances for expeditions aimed at claiming captives or scalps as opposed to livestock or other booty. The Apache, who usually tried to avoid combat when stealing horses or other prizes, performed their war dance only when they intended to take violent revenge on their enemies. Like other tribes, they used the occasion to evoke the passions of battle and strengthen the commitment of the individual warrior to the group and its guiding spirits. Men danced to the songs of a shaman. When the shaman sang a warrior's name, that man was honor-bound to dance and join the war party, regardless of what his own instincts might be telling him.

An Apache war dance usually concluded with women joining in. The messenger who traveled from camp to camp announcing the dances assured the men that there would be no sexual indiscretions. He asked the men to ''loan'' their wives for the night. ''She can dance with a man, but she will return to you just as she left you," the messenger might say. "Even if she is dancing with another man and talking with him, it means nothing. The same way with girls. They will come back in the morning."

When the time for departure drew near, the warriors might set up a new camp, in order to signal their withdrawal from the community, or they might sequester themselves at the dwelling of their chief. The night before a Pawnee war party set out, the leader summoned his warriors to meet at his lodge with their supplies. They all sat up late into the night, recounting past feats: Anyone who fell asleep during the tales would be dropped from the expedition. At dawn the warriors left the camp, the leader at their head bearing a sacred pipe in his left hand. The Pipe Holder, as the war leader was known, commanded the complete obedience of his followers.

On the trail, as in the village, proper conduct was essential to the successful completion of the endeavor. Warriors everywhere would safeguard their relationship with the sacred powers by observing taboos until they resumed the path of peace. Ritual governed the way the men ate and slept, even the language they used. "On the warpath there were special words that had to be used," an Apache fighting man recalled; "a horse was called by a different word; a woman was; a Mexican was also." In such coded speech as in his way of fighting, the Apache warrior tended to be subtle and indirect: A mule was referred to by a phrase meaning "shakes his tail," while water was called "it keeps moving."

Untested members of an Ojibwa war party were cautioned never to step over a warrior's weapons laid side by side on the ground, lest they sap the powerful medicine of the weapons. At sunset of each day on the trail, the men drank a strength-enhancing potion; then the veteran fighters chanted their personal war songs, one after another. A solemn, subdued version of the War Dance followed, with each member partaking of the potion. In the morning, before setting out, they smoked a war pipe to keep faith with the spirits as the moment of truth approached.

A Plains pipe holder paid close attention to his dreams along the war trail, looking for tactical insights into the coming battle, such as the location and size of the enemy's encampment, or the terrain where the clash would occur. Upon reaching enemy territory, he led a ceremony in which each warrior smoked the sacred pipe and meditated on the contents of his personal medicine bundle. The Pipe Holder prayed for the expedition's

Reenacting a war ritual, two Apache scouts apply traditional war paint in a photograph taken around 1885. Warriors preparing for battle painted their faces, some choosing colors and designs they had seen in a vision. The marking served either to identify the individual during the fight or to indicate the warrior society to which he belonged.

success, while other warriors sacrificed favorite possessions or tiny bits of their own flesh.

Even the reports of scouts were considered occasions for ceremony. When Blackfeet warriors were off on a raid, for example, they would pile up sticks while waiting for scouts to return. When they appeared, the war leader kicked over the pile, and a wild scramble for the scattered sticks ensued. The Blackfeet believed that each stick a warrior recovered represented a horse he would capture in the upcoming raid.

For the majority of Native American fighting men, the final hours before a raid or battle were marked by fresh appeals to patron spirits and renewed pledges of steadfastness to one's comrades. Many men donned full regalia just before entering combat to acquire the powerful medicine embodied in the clothing, to display their prowess to the enemy, and to be properly attired for entry into the spirit world should they be killed in battle. Other Indian warriors stripped down to a breechcloth for action, invoking their war medicine by painting their bodies lavishly. Among the Cheyenne, the climactic ritual was the donning of the war bonnet. Chanting a special song, the warrior raised the feathers toward the sun four times before securing the headdress and taking up his weapons.

The success of a war party did not rest entirely on the ritual observances of the fighting men. Much depended on the conduct of their neighbors and kin back home. Among Plains Indians, it was common for at least one shaman to remain behind in the village and pray for the warriors' success and safe return. In order to keep the men in the thoughts of the people, he rode through the village periodically, shouting their names.

Among the Mohave, by contrast, villagers considered it bad medicine to think or talk about the warriors except on the day when the fighting was supposed to begin.

Indian women bore special responsibilities for the spiritual welfare of their men while they were away on the warpath. Young unmarried Mandan women fasted in support of their warriors and passed the days praying for victory. Each morning at dawn, the maidens went separately from their village into the surrounding hills, where they would cry out invocations to the spirits. They maintained their solitary vigils all day, keeping a prayerful attitude as they did quill work or performed other quiet tasks. In parts of the Pacific Northwest, when a war party left its village, it was customary for the women to prepare lifelike dolls fashioned out of animal skins stuffed with grass and brush. Every morning the women sought to transmit death-dealing power to the distant fighters by taking up ceremonial wooden knives and attacking the dolls as if they were the enemy. In addition, married women wore ornate belts for the duration of the expedition. A woman who untied her belt could be held responsible for any misfortune that befell the war party. Symbolic of chastity, the belts may also have helped to prevent jealousy on the part of the distant warriors.

Apache wives were expected to pray for their warrior husbands every morning for four days—as well as every time they pulled a pot of stew off the fire. They also were required to keep children away from the woodpiles; any scattering of the logs portended death. Some wives, however, supported the men more directly by accompanying them to battle. Leaving their children with grandparents, these women prepared food for their husbands, tended the wounded, and performed other duties. Some-

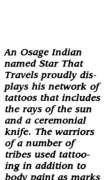

An Osage Indian named Star That Travels proudly displays his network of tattoos that includes the rays of the sun and a ceremonial knife. The warriors of a number of tribes used tattooing in addition to body paint as marks of distinction.

times they even participated in ambushes and attacks. One Apache woman by the name of Lozen became a respected warrior in her own right. The close relative of an Apache chief, she learned early on how to ride and rope—useful skills for the tribe's frequent horse raids. When she finally put her skills to the test, she proved to be the Apache answer at cutting out enemy horses and stampeding herds. Although Lozen never married, she was invited to accompany the men on raids and demonstrated a genius for locating enemy forces and eluding them. The Apache still tell of the time when she found herself deep in enemy territory with a young Apache mother and her baby. Forgoing her own chance for a quick escape, she led the woman and child on a grueling journey to safety that took several months. Such was her reputation among the people that in 1886, the Apache chose her as a go-between to negotiate the surrender of Geronimo's band to United States forces.

An Ojibwa named Chief Earth Woman won similar renown for her martial exploits, which began when she decided to follow her lover on a

The Osage tattooing implements below include a clamshell to hold dyes and a half-dozen sharp metal needles, used for pricking the skin, that are decorated with rushes, feathers, and tiny brass bells. The tools were stored in a rolled-up woven mat that was itself a sacred object, made by women who fasted while they did the weaving. It was a matter of honor among warriors not to show pain during the tattooing process.

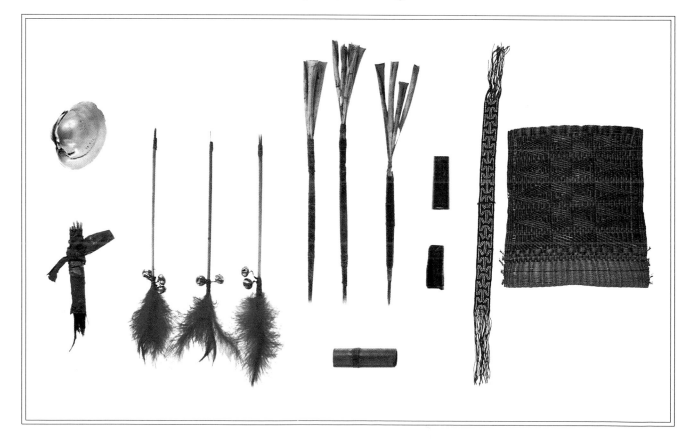

war party against the neighboring Sioux. Ojibwa women traditionally accompanied the departing warriors some distance away from the village, but on one occasion, Chief Earth Woman did not turn back with the others. Instead, she persuaded the war leader to allow her to join the war party, telling him of supernatural powers that had been conferred on her in a dream. She demonstrated her worth by predicting enemy movements, allowing the Ojibwas to overtake the Sioux. When the Ojibwas fell upon the surprised foe, Chief Earth Woman took the scalp of the first fallen Sioux, slain by her lover. At the victory celebration that followed, she received the same honors accorded to all new warriors.

While a war party was away, the rest of the community waited anxiously for the safe return of their warriors. Typically, the long, tense vigil was broken by the arrival of a runner heralding the party's approach. If there had been casualties, the warriors might stop outside the village to give bereaved relatives time to prepare themselves for the return ceremonies. If the losses had been heavy, the warriors considered the raid to have been a failure. They might even discard their scalps and other booty. When Crow raiders returned from such a defeat, they stopped far from home and sent a messenger to a prominent place near the village, where he signaled news of the defeat and the number of men lost by firing a gun or waving a robe. The messenger was then visited by a party of elders, who received the full story of the setback and returned to the village to lead the community in mourning. The warriors remained in seclusion for 10 days, then began gathering provisions for another foray to avenge the earlier losses.

The return of a successful war party, however, was a joyous occasion. Losses still had to be mourned, of course, but for most of the tribe, there were new honors to celebrate and fresh spoils to distribute. When victorious Assiniboin warriors returned to their camp, one member of the party signaled the achievement by trotting his pony on a zigzag course. People ran from the camp to accept scalps, horses, and other booty, handed out by warriors in a euphoric flush of generosity.

Successful Pawnee warriors prepared for their triumphal entry by painting themselves and their ponies. Four men thus decorated rode back and forth on a hill overlooking the village. When all eyes had turned to the painted riders, the rest of the war party joined them on the bluff, whooping and singing war songs. Emissaries rode out to meet the war-

A plume of eagle feathers decorates a Mandan communal pipe, with a 46-inch stem, that was collected by Lewis and Clark on their expedition of 1804 1806. In many tribes, a warrior planning a raid or an attack on an enemy group would recruit volunteers for the mission while carrying a pipe around his village. Those fellow tribesmen who agreed to join the war party smoked the pipe to signify their willingness.

riors, whose leader related the number of opponents killed, coups counted, scalps taken, and horses captured. The messengers took the news back to the camp, followed at a distance by the war party, who stopped at the outskirts to distribute the captured horses to relatives and the village chief. Before returning to their lodges, those warriors who had taken scalps during the battle turned them over to the medicine man who had helped them prepare their war bundles.

For a number of tribes, captives were an important component of the spoils of war, and in some instances, captured warriors met an excruciating demise. The practice of torture, which was sometimes followed by the ceremonial eating of part of the victim's organs or flesh, allowed the entire tribe to partake of revenge and symbolically incorporate the enemy's power and spirit. For the captives, torture was the ultimate test of courage; warriors tried to keep from crying out, opening their lips only to sing their death song. If they did so, even their tormentors would acknowledge that they had died well.

Jesuit missionaries who ventured among the Iroquois in the 17th cen-

THE PROTECTIVE POWER OF THE TALISMAN

No Indian warrior entered into battle without taking along his personal talisman. These tokens, frequently shaped like shields, assured the wearers that their guardian spirits were present, bringing with them the supernatural power needed for victory.

The talismans not only bolstered the warriors' courage, they were also believed to give a fighter's arm added strength and to deflect enemy arrows. In addition, amulets that were worn prominently in the hair or around the neck served as a warning to foes that they faced not just human opponents but also the omnipotent spirits.

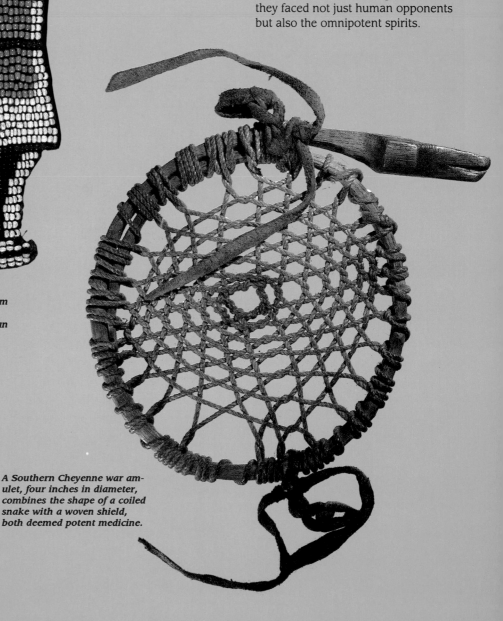

Two human figures made of beads with a brass tack between them form a talisman once worn by a warrior of the northern Plains' Piegan tribe as a hair ornament.

A Southern Cheyenne war amulet, four inches in diameter, combines the shape of a coiled snake with a woven shield, both deemed potent medicine.

Metal gun parts—bits of triggers and hammers—decorate the necklace of this Arapaho war charm. The spider-web-like disk was designed to "capture" the enemy.

The complex talisman worn by a Crow warrior includes a shield bearing a human figure, some owl feathers, and a beaded symbol with braided human hair attached.

tury witnessed torture frequently—and occasionally experienced it first-hand. Chief among the torturers, according to Jesuit accounts, was a stern leader of the Onondaga Iroquois named Aharihon, renowned among his people as a great warrior. Aharihon's brother died about 1654 at the hands of the rival Erie, a tribe to the west of the Iroquois League. Aharihon undertook to avenge his brother's death—an obligation that could be met either by killing one or more of the enemy or by adopting a captive to take the dead man's place. Within a few years of his brother's death, Aharihon had considered some 40 prisoners for adoption, his own captives as well as those presented to him by other warriors. None was worthy to take his brother's place, he decided, so each prisoner was roasted to death over a slow fire.

A Jesuit priest named Father Lalemant witnessed the reception of one captured candidate for adoption and recorded the events that followed. Aharihon first assuaged the young man's fears, presenting him with four dogs with which to prepare a feast to celebrate his adoption. The feast was well under way, with the captive rejoicing and singing to his guests, when Aharihon arose and announced to the company that this captive, too, was unfit and thus must die. "The poor lad was astounded at this," Father Lalemant wrote, "and turned toward the door to make his escape, but was stopped by two men who had orders to burn him." The plan was to roast the prisoner slowly from the feet to the waist during the evening, then let him regain strength until daybreak, when the rekindled fire would finish the job. The stunned victim had no time to gather courage, however, and he did not go quietly. His cries and groans aroused the pity of one of Aharihon's relatives, who first besought the chief to kill the youth with a knife, and finally persuaded him to continue the fire uninter-rupted, ending the victim's suffering by dawn.

Aharihon continued his career of retribution for several more years, tallying each victim with a fresh tattoo on his thigh. By 1663 he was well marked, having slain 60 men with his own hand and ordered 80 more burned. But while the French at Montreal called him Nero for his cruelty, his own people considered him a stern but capable leader. Each death he inflicted, they reasoned, was a rightful expression of respect for his dead brother. His devotion to his brother's memory contributed to Aharihon's reputation as a man of resolve, one who could be trusted as an ambas-sador on important missions to negotiate with the French.

Although prominent warriors such as Aharihon could determine the fate of their own captives, Iroquois women generally had a strong say in

Made of leather and decorated with bird and porcupine quills, feathers, and various roots, this sash served as an insignia of the Chey-enne tribe's pres-tigious Dog Soldier Society. The warrior wearing it around his neck would drive a lance through the trailing end when battle was joined as a vow to stand fast unless released by his comrades.

Off on the warpath

A Cheyenne raiding party attired in full war regalia rides out from a village in a drawing done by a tribesman named Making Medicine. Considered to be among the most assertive of the Plains tribes, the Cheyenne were consummate horse raiders.

the disposition of prisoners, as they did in most tribal decisions. A captive was often assigned to a family, whose matriarch could decree adoption, enslavement, or torture. Male prisoners selected for adoption often had to run a gantlet composed of women and children armed with whips. If the men stayed on their feet, they were welcomed into the tribe, taking on all the privileges and obligations of the dead people they replaced. In periods of prolonged, bloody warfare, more than half the population of some Iroquois villages consisted of adopted captives.

Adoption was also common among the Sioux. Warriors accepted captive children into their own families, treating them the same as their own. A captured woman might be allowed to choose between marrying

her captor and being sent back to her people. In the hope of winning a wife, Sioux warriors sometimes kept a sharp eye out during raids for attractive females. Men, however, were considered too dangerous to keep, and were usually killed rather than captured.

Female captives generally did not have to fear rape, at least in the first weeks of their captivity, because warriors were normally obliged to remain celibate as part of their purification rituals following battles. And while women sometimes participated in the torture of captives, as prisoners they were less likely to suffer it. "Women and children do not make good charcoal" was the conventional wisdom of the Gros Ventre of Montana, who preferred the course of adoption, especially into families that had been left childless by war or illness.

In some tribes, the adoption process was complicated by the fact that

Santiago McKinn, an Irish-Mexican boy captured by the Apache, stands with a group of Indian children in Geronimo's Skeleton Canyon encampment in 1886. All captives were deemed spoils of war; some were killed or made slaves, but most were treated well and adopted into a tribe, taking the place of members lost in battle or through disease. McKinn was later freed during negotiations between the Apache and the U.S. Army.

the prisoners were considered to be spiritually dangerous. Mohave shamans purified captives by carefully washing them four mornings in a row. During that time, the prisoners had to abide by the same dietary restrictions as the returning warriors, who could eat no meat or salt. Even a purified female captive was not considered a fit match for a Mohave warrior, however. Such women were usually given as wives to older men. The Cocopah of the Southwest put more trust in their purification rites. When a Cocopah couple received a captive child, they were obliged to bathe the youngster daily at a riverbank with water warmed in a large clay jug. Thus cleansed of taint, the adopted children were generally so well treated that few ever tried to escape.

Ritual washing also was part of the adoption ceremonies of the Caughnawaga, a branch of the Mohawk and members of the Iroquois League. Colonist James Smith was 18 years old in 1755 when the Caughnawaga captured him while he was helping to build a road in western Pennsylvania. Smith, who lived for four years among the Indians before returning to white society, later described how three Caughnawaga women dunked him in the Allegheny River in order to transform him into an Indian: "One of the chiefs made a speech, which was delivered to me by an interpreter—and was as follows: 'My son, you are now flesh of our flesh, and bone of our bone. By this ceremony which was performed this day, every drop of white blood was washed out of your veins; you are taken into the Caughnawaga nation, and initiated into a warlike tribe; you are adopted into a great family.' "

Like the captives, returning warriors were required to undergo purification rites in order to rid themselves of the dangerous influence of the enemy and to smooth the transition from the violence of the battlefield to the peace of village life. These ceremonies were frequently quite elaborate, as was the case with those witnessed by a white trader named James Adair upon the return of a Chickasaw war party in 1765. A day's march from home, the Chickasaw war leader dispatched a runner to carry the tidings of victory to the village, and to order that his winter house, where the warriors had gathered before their departure, be swept clean to prevent spiritual pollution. The women of the tribe had already cleaned the house thoroughly when the war party set off, leaving the sweepings in a heap behind the door until the messenger brought the order to remove them. Every utensil that had been used by women during the leader's absence was also removed from the house.

When the warriors appeared the next day, they were painted red and black, with a tuft of long white feathers atop their heads, which were also covered with swansdown. They approached the camp carrying the scalps of two men on pine branches, solemnly intoning what Adair called a death song, punctuated by shrill whoops. The leader then danced and sang his way around his house, Adair noted, appealing to the tribe's Great Spirit and "ascribing the victory over their enemies to his strong arm, instead of their own." After receiving assurances that the house had been properly prepared, the leader led his company inside to begin three days and nights of isolation. As they had done before their departure, they took no food between dawn and dusk, drinking only the purifying snake-root brew and rubbing themselves down with lotions around the fire. Every two to three hours, the warriors emerged to circle a red-painted war pole erected before the house, waving the pine boughs with the trophy scalps before reentering the house.

Traditionally, the women of the village played an important role in the victory ritual. Each night the female relatives of the warriors arrayed themselves in two facing rows outside the door of the war leader's house. Bathed, anointed, and wearing their finest clothes, they stood throughout the night, singing a victory song. Between songs, they waited in perfect silence. For the duration of the purification period, they observed numerous taboos, including abstention from salt.

When the three days had elapsed, the men and women bathed separately, then joined in a procession to the houses of families who had lost relatives to the enemy. The war leader went first, followed by his attendant, then the warriors, and finally the singers; at each stop, they pinned a small piece of a scalp to the top of the house with a pine twig. "This order they observed from house to house," Adair wrote, "till in their opinion they had appeased the ghosts of their dead." When the last bit of scalp was distributed, everyone in the procession bathed again, ending the ceremony for all but the leader and his assistant, who remained in isolation for an additional three days.

For the Maricopa along the Gila River in Arizona, the purification ritual began on the journey home. Men who had been contaminated by killing, scalping, or capturing an enemy traveled in single file behind the main body of warriors. They maintained perfect silence on the march and observed numerous restrictions, including one against spitting on the ground, lest pursuing enemy spirits come in contact with the spittle and

Crow warriors rest and bathe on the bank of a river near their camp in the northern Plains in an 1834 George Catlin painting. The warriors of many Indian groups bathed ceremonially following a raid or battle to rid themselves of the enemies' taint and to mark the transition from war to peace.

acquire the influence to make them ill. At night they camped separately, and received little food or drink. When they reached the outskirts of their territory, they purged themselves by drinking large quantities of water and allowing an older warrior to run an arrowweed stalk down their throats until they vomited. Then they bathed in the river.

Thus began a period of 16 days of isolation. In the village, a hut built hastily after a runner brought word of the battle's outcome awaited each warrior. The man remained in his hut for the duration of the period, bathing daily before dawn, then consuming the day's only meal, a small portion of mesquite bean gruel. For eight nights in the middle of the period they daubed their heads, using mud mixed with boiled mesquite bark for four nights, then mud alone for four more. Old warriors visited the men every evening to remind them of their obligations. The elders exhorted their listeners to resist the approach of enemy spirits, to eschew laziness, theft, and begging, and to treat others with kindness.

A man who had taken an enemy scalp kept it with him during the isolation period. When he finally emerged from the hut, he presented the scalp to a former warrior, designated as the keeper of scalps, who stored it with others in a large jar in the tribal meeting house. Before dawn on the 16th night, the warrior left his hut to return to his own dwelling. En-

Carrying his spear and shield, his body painted with ornate symbols, an aged Sioux warrior named Last Horse appears ready for battle in a photograph taken at a large Indian congress in 1898. The days of tribal warfare had vanished, but Last Horse did take part in a mock battle staged during the assembly.

tering just as the sun rose, he went directly to the rear, where he sat with his back to his family. The warrior could now eat when his family did, but he was not allowed to shift his position except to sleep or to take his dawn baths. Four more days would pass before the malignant powers of the enemy were considered to be utterly exhausted. Only at that time was the warrior permitted to join the rest of the tribe.

When the warriors moved from their huts to their homes and surrendered the scalps they had taken, the Maricopa celebrated with a scalp dance, performed by the old men and women of the tribe. The scalps, tied on hoops and decorated in the Maricopa style, were mounted on a tall pole by the Scalp Keeper. Women formed a circle around the pole, their faces painted to look like those of warriors with masklike black stripes across the eyes. Hands joined, they moved counterclockwise around the pole, reaching down occasionally for handfuls of dirt to throw at the scalps. As they mimed their own scalps being taken, their mocking cries were joined by those of the old men gathered outside the circle. The dance lasted all day. At dusk, the scalps were moved to a shorter post just inside the doorway of the meeting house. There the elderly celebrants joined in a variety of songs and chants, accompanying themselves with rattles or by beating and scraping overturned baskets. At the conclusion of the nightlong singing, the trophies were returned to the Scalp Keeper, who put them into the large pot with the rest of the tribe's scalps.

For many tribes, victory celebrations led to wider festivities. The Cheyenne, for example, began their ceremonies with a scalp dance, but soon progressed to dances that allowed young people to pair off with their sweethearts. These affairs were presided over by males who dressed as old men but had taken up the ways of women. These "halfmen-halfwomen," as they were called, were respected as fine talkers and matchmakers, and often served as intermediaries for the young people. Warriors, too, sought their company, frequently inviting them on war expeditions, as they made entertaining companions and were skilled in treating the wounded. After a battle, the halfmen-halfwomen received the best scalps, which they carried into the village at the ends of poles—usually at dawn, for greatest effect.

The Scalp Dance took place in the evening, around a great fire made from wood that had been provided by every lodge in the village. The halfmen-halfwomen took up position nearest the fire, holding the scalps aloft on their poles. Around them in a square stood the rest of the tribe, with singers carrying drums and middle-aged married men on one side,

Osage Indians, in ritual finery, prepare to enter the wooden lodge behind them to perform a war dance in honor of their brave heritage. By 1890, when the photograph was taken, the era of tribal warfare was over, and the Osage had signed treaties with the United States. (The American flag on the roof was raised upside down by mistake.)

and the old men and mature women opposite them. The other two sides of the square were composed of rows of young men and women of courtship age, facing each other across the fire. The celebration started with the young men moving across the square to join the girls for an arm-in-arm sweetheart dance. At the end of this brief dance, the young people returned to their rows, and the halfmen-halfwomen began to dance before the drummers along with the mature women, waving the scalp poles in the air. The fathers of successful warriors danced nearby, often clowning to make the people laugh.

The next event was a matchmaking dance, in which the halfmen-halfwomen first consulted the wishes of the young men and women as to their preference of partner, then paired off the couples as best they could. Succeeding dances allowed the young people to choose their partners directly, and to come closer together. The halfmen-halfwomen danced around the outside, waving the scalps to frighten away children who crowded too close. The dancing grew wilder as the night progressed. It ended only with the dawn, as the people returned to their homes full of life, with the trials of warfare far from their minds.

The vibrancy and power of the age-old purification ceremonies remain strong today. In the late 1960s and early 1970s, some Indian combat veterans returning from the war in Vietnam found their readjustment to peacetime society made easier because of the rituals and songs that endured among certain tribes. Concerned about their son's psychological wounds, the family of one Navajo soldier, for example, had a medicine man conduct an Enemyway ritual to protect him from the ghosts of the enemy dead and to exorcise the violence of the battlefield. The ancient ceremony restored the young man to a state of harmony with the world. "It snapped me out of it," he later declared.

A Kiowa veteran experienced a similar sense of renewal after a tribal feast given in tribute to his military service. "My people honored me as a warrior," he recalled. "My parents and grandparents thanked everyone who prayed for my safe return. As we circled the drum, I got a feeling of pride. I felt good inside because that's the way the Kiowa people tell you that you've done well." True to their heritage, Native Americans celebrated their young fighting men for having gained through war a maturity and a wisdom far beyond their years. "We honor our veterans for their bravery," a Winnebago elder explained, "and because by seeing death on the battlefield they truly know the greatness of life."

Navajo volunteers
are sworn into the
Marine Corps at
Fort Wingate, New
Mexico, in October
1942. At the time,
an army official not-
ed that "if the en-
tire population en-
listed in the same
proportion as Indi-
ans, there would
be no need for se-
lective service."

FINDING HONOR IN THE MILITARY

On December 7, 1941, the superintend-ent of the Navajo Indian Reservation at Window Rock, Arizona, saw a crowd of armed young men assembling out-side his office. When asked why they had come, they answered: "We're going to fight."

The Navajos' resolve to join in the conflict followed a long tradition of Indians serving in the U.S. armed forces. In the 19th century, white en-croachments on Indian territory prevented tribes from fighting their ancestral enemies. The ranks of warrior societies thinned, and young men could not fulfill the ancient prerequisites for leadership through warfare.

Military service provided a substitute for traditional

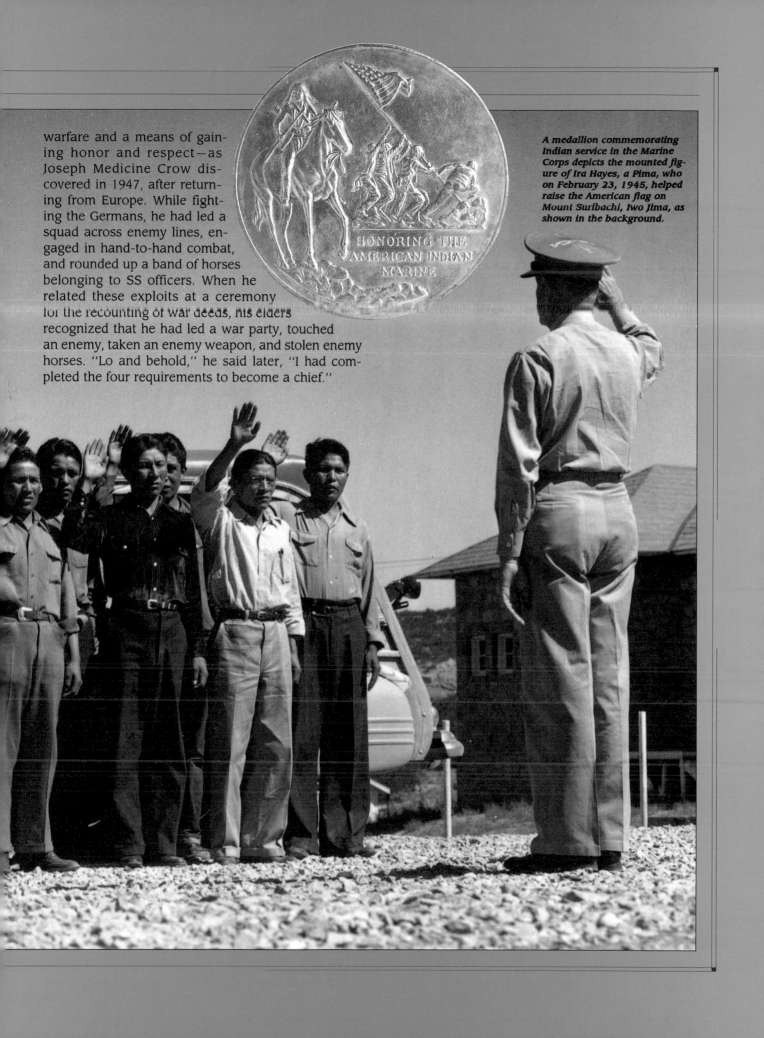

warfare and a means of gaining honor and respect—as Joseph Medicine Crow discovered in 1947, after returning from Europe. While fighting the Germans, he had led a squad across enemy lines, engaged in hand-to-hand combat, and rounded up a band of horses belonging to SS officers. When he related these exploits at a ceremony for the recounting of war deeds, his elders recognized that he had led a war party, touched an enemy, taken an enemy weapon, and stolen enemy horses. "Lo and behold," he said later, "I had completed the four requirements to become a chief."

A medallion commemorating Indian service in the Marine Corps depicts the mounted figure of Ira Hayes, a Pima, who on February 23, 1945, helped raise the American flag on Mount Suribachi, Iwo Jima, as shown in the background.

HONORING THE
AMERICAN INDIAN
MARINE

SOLDIERING IN THE CIVIL WAR

Units that were composed entirely of Native Americans served as auxiliary troops to the armies on both sides during the Civil War. Drawn principally from the Five Civilized Nations—the Choctaw, Cherokee, Seminole, Creek, and Chickasaw of Indian Territory in present-day Oklahoma—they served largely in the western border states, winning respect that helped pave the way for their acceptance into the postwar military. "The officers and soldiers of our own regiments now freely acknowledge them to be valuable allies," wrote a Union officer in an 1862 battlefield dispatch. "The prejudice once existing against them is fast disappearing from our army."

Two Indians raise their hands to be sworn into a Wisconsin volunteer militia serving the Union cause. Although the U.S. Army was generally reluctant to induct Indians into the regular ranks, local militias often recruited them.

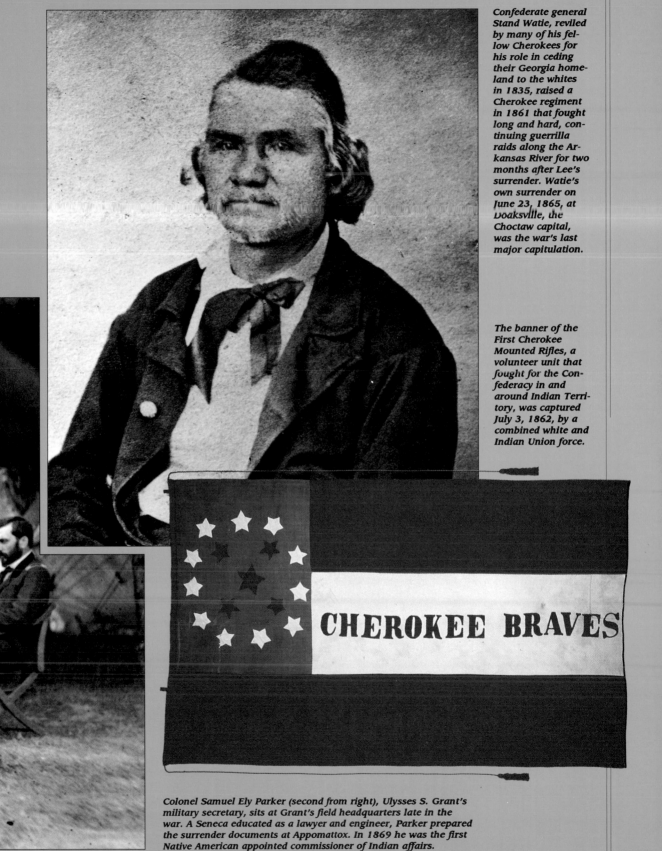

Confederate general Stand Watie, reviled by many of his fellow Cherokees for his role in ceding their Georgia homeland to the whites in 1835, raised a Cherokee regiment in 1861 that fought long and hard, continuing guerrilla raids along the Arkansas River for two months after Lee's surrender. Watie's own surrender on June 23, 1865, at Doaksville, the Choctaw capital, was the war's last major capitulation.

The banner of the First Cherokee Mounted Rifles, a volunteer unit that fought for the Confederacy in and around Indian Territory, was captured July 3, 1862, by a combined white and Indian Union force.

CHEROKEE BRAVES

Colonel Samuel Ely Parker (second from right), Ulysses S. Grant's military secretary, sits at Grant's field headquarters late in the war. A Seneca educated as a lawyer and engineer, Parker prepared the surrender documents at Appomattox. In 1869 he was the first Native American appointed commissioner of Indian affairs.

SCOUTING WITH THE BLUECOATS

During the Indian Wars, the army instituted a policy of enlisting Indian scouts as regular troops. As General George Crook observed, "to polish a diamond, there is nothing like its own dust"—a maxim borne out by his own 1872-1874 Apache campaign, in which Indian units killed 272 Apaches and captured 313 more. Units that did not include Indians accounted for fewer than 20 hostiles killed or captured.

Indians had many motives for joining the bluecoats, from striking back at old enemies to feeding their families. Some pragmatically picked the winning side. Said Chief Blackfoot of the Crow, "We want our reservation to be large; we want to go on eating buffalo, and so we hold fast to the whites."

The Apache scout Alchesay (second from left, center row) received the Medal of Honor for serving with Crook against rival Apaches. He was later instrumental in capturing the Apache leader Geronimo.

Oglala Sioux scouts clad in army blue drill at South Dakota's Pine Ridge reservation in 1890. Despite lingering hostility toward Indian recruits, white unit commanders prized their services and begged for permission to enlist more of them. Wrote an officer to Washington in 1867, "They are all but indispensable."

This guidon, emblazoned with a bow and crossed arrows, was issued by the army in 1890 to Company A of the U.S. Scouts, an Indian unit that served in the Dakotas.

Five Choctaw infantrymen (with their captain, at extreme right) were among the fluent Choctaw speakers employed as Code Talkers in the Meuse-Argonne campaign of 1918.

The Choctaw nation's Medal of Valour was commissioned to honor the tribe's World War I Code Talkers. Its design features the nation's great seal, with a pipe hatchet, arrows, and an unstrung bow.

SPECIAL DUTY IN THE GREAT WAR

More than 10,000 Indians served in the U.S. military during the First World War. Although no longer set apart in all-Indian units, most were concentrated in outfits drawn from the National Guard of states with large Indian populations. And officers of those units sometimes grouped Indians together for special duties in the belief that they had natural gifts, such as an affinity for tracking or a talent for marksmanship.

However valid those assumptions, Indian soldiers did have one valuable and unique attribute: their impenetrable native languages. In units such as Oklahoma's 142d Infantry, with its sizable Choctaw contingent, Indian Code Talkers speaking by telephone easily confounded German eavesdroppers who had tapped Allied lines.

Too old to enlist legally, Corporal George Miner lied about his age to join the army with a group of fellow Winnebagos and fight in the First World War.

A horse-drawn reel-cart manned by an all-Indian crew lays communications wire in a training exercise at Fort Riley, Kansas. Nicknamed the All-American Team, the crew of Sioux, Apache, and Comanche Indians was assembled by an officer from members of tribes known for their horsemanship.

A PASSION FOR THE FRAY

Expressing a disdain shared by thousands of Native Americans at the start of World War II, a Blackfeet Indian said of the Selective Service System: "Since when has it been necessary for Blackfeet to draw lots to fight?" True to those sentiments, more than half the eligible residents of some reservations volunteered for military service. Eventually, as many as 40,000 Indians went to war out of a population of 400,000.

Indians have continued to contribute mightily to America's fighting forces up to the present day. The proportion of Native Americans serving in Vietnam was significantly higher than that of the population as a whole. Like other soldiers, Indian veterans have sometimes returned to find the nation seemingly indifferent to their sacrifice. But among their own people, they receive the same honor accorded their warrior ancestors. Declared Max Little, a Seminole who saw combat in Vietnam: "Our veterans are never forgotten."

Two of the Marines' 420 Navajo Code Talkers, who relayed information in the Pacific during World War II, operate a portable radio in a jungle clearing. Japanese cryptographers never deciphered the code, based on an unwritten language spoken by fewer than 30 people outside the Navajo nation.

Lieutenant Ernest Childers (above) receives the Medal of Honor for his actions in the 1943 Italian campaign. The Oklahoma Creek was one of five Indians awarded the nation's highest military honor in World War II. His division, the 45th Infantry—praised by General George Patton as one of the best "in the history of American arms"—drew troops from Oklahoma, New Mexico, Arizona, and Colorado. The region's Indian heritage was reflected in the unit shoulder patch (right) depicting a thunderbird.

REBIRTH OF THE BLACK LEGS

Two hundred years ago, when the Kiowa ruled with the Comanche as lords of the southern Plains, Kiowa society contained a hierarchy of men's military organizations. Nearly all were extinct by the early 20th century. Then in 1958, a group of Kiowa veterans met at a VFW hall in Carnegie, Oklahoma, and revived one of their tribe's oldest warrior societies, the *Tonkonga,* or "Black Legs."

According to one legend, the name dates from before the time the Kiowa acquired horses. Warriors then would return from raids with their legs blackened by dust from the trail. Later, they painted their legs black for ceremonies.

Today's Black Legs cleave to their heritage. While other Indian military societies have relaxed their entrance requirements, the Tonkonga accept only men who have served in the armed forces. At their twice-yearly ceremonies, shown on these pages, they honor veterans with songs and dances taught by tribal elders.

"You younger men are entitled to carry it on," Kiowa elders told World War II veteran Gus Palmer, who revived the Tonkonga to honor his brother and others who died in combat. "You men today are just like the men in the old days, warriors. You fought for your people."

The Black Legs' ceremonial tipi is painted with a striped design from the famous battle tipi of Dohausen, Kiowa tribal chief from 1833 to 1866, the crests of modern military divisions, and the names of Kiowa servicemen killed in America's 20th-century wars.

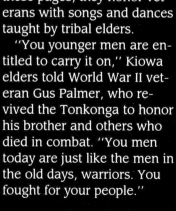

George Neconie
Pacific

Joe Gouladdle
Pacific

Lyndreth L Palmer
Germany

Matthew Hawzita
Germany

Luke Tainpeah
Korea

Silas Boyidde
Korea

Donald Bear
Viet-Nam

Cletus Poolaw
Viet-Nam

Members of the Tonkonga Society parade onto the dance ground at the start of their fall ceremony. The Tonkonga today are sometimes called Black Leggings for the garments they wear instead of painting their legs black as their ancestors did.

Following an opening prayer and song, members of the Kiowa women's Veteran's Auxiliary perform a victory dance while the men prepare for the coming ceremonies (left). Blue blankets are worn by the War Mothers chapter, whose members have all sent relatives into military service.

Women's auxiliary member Vanessa Morgan wears a traditional Kiowa woman's buckskin dress. Her son, Gabe, standing next to her, is covered in the striking black and yellow paint long worn by the Black Legs.

Carrying the men's lances, female relatives of Tonkonga Society members perform the Scalp Dance, held to welcome men home from war. Kiowa women have traditionally gained prestige through the feats of their men as well as through their own skills.

The founding commander of the revived society, Gus Palmer (flanked by brothers George and Dixon), holds a lance adorned with 21 eagle feathers commemorating his 21 World War II bombing missions. The red capes, which are worn by all Tonkonga members, represent the cape that the Palmers' great-grandfather, Gool-hay-ee, captured from a Mexican officer.

Toward the end of the fall ceremony's final dance, a combat veteran selected for the honor—in this instance, the man walking behind those in the war bonnets at far left—calls for the drum to stop. He then recites a personal coup or a battle deed. Tonkonga members have served in every major United States conflict from World War I through Desert Storm.

Resting between dances, the men sit with their lances thrust into the ground and await the next song. Dances are performed in sets during the weekend-long ceremony.

The Black Legs gather at the 1990 fall ceremony in which the army's night combat helicopter, the OH-58D, received the official name Kiowa Warrior. Upon being presented with a photograph of the aircraft (inset), society commander Gus Palmer said, "It is indeed appropriate that our Kiowa warriors be honored by such a fearsome weapon that fights at night and protects our country with the same dedication as our society's members."

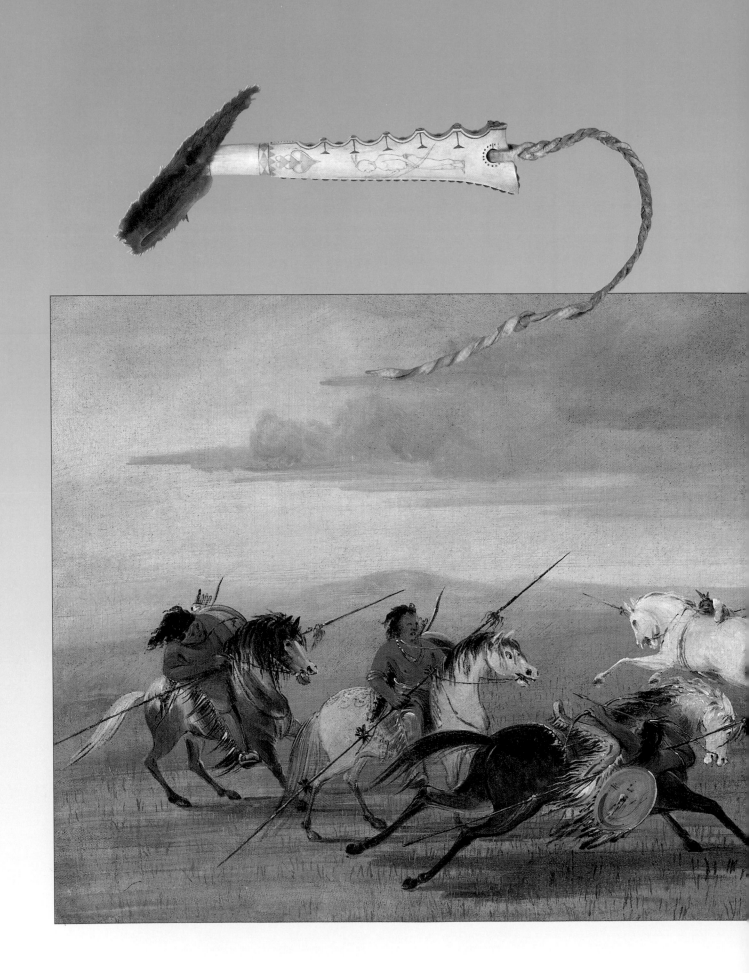

3

THE TACTICS OF DECEPTION AND DARING

"He will hang whilst his horse is at full speed, carrying with him his bow . . . which he will wield upon his enemy as he passes," wrote an awe-struck George Catlin of the warriors in the Comanche sham battle he depicted in this 1835 painting. Horsemen of all tribes carried quirts, like the Osage one above, to urge on their mounts.

Among the Ottawa Indians of the Great Lakes region as among many other Native American peoples, war was declared with resounding ceremony but executed with quiet determination. "Take courage, young men," an Ottawa chief would exhort his followers when the time for action drew near. "Crop your hair, put on your war paint, fill your quivers, and let us console our dead. Let our war songs reecho through the village, awaken our brother who was slain; he will be content when he has been avenged." Such defiant words and the clamor they raised set the stage for a methodical act of retribution. Relating the sequence of events was the French explorer Antoine de la Mothe Cadillac, who founded the outpost of Detroit in 1701 and dealt extensively with the Ottawa. The raid he described—carried out to avenge losses inflicted by the enemy—was typical in many ways of tribal hostilities before European contact changed Indian warfare significantly.

Once the Ottawa warriors who answered the chief's call had uttered their oaths and sung their war songs, Cadillac noted, they bent to their task with great composure. "When they have reached the enemy's country, they go warily," he wrote. "They keep silence, observe everything, and never shoot firearms. If they come upon the trail of any persons, they can easily distinguish whether it is old or recent; they know the number of people who have passed there, and how many days ago their journey was made; and, as they know when their enemy went by, they can tell pretty nearly where they will be."

Like other white men who marveled at Indian tracking skills, Cadillac found it hard to believe that the Ottawa acquired such abilities through practice and diligence, as all scouts must. "One might say that these people are guided by instinct rather than by knowledge or reason," he speculated, "for if a man or a number of men are discovered, their doom is almost certain and unfailing. It is in vain to try to escape; you may walk on moss or leaves, or through marshes, or even over rocks, but all precautions you take to conceal your track are quite useless, for the pursuers are rarely at fault. The strangest thing is that they know by the impress of the foot, or its shape, to what tribe the people in front of them belong."

Having tracked their quarry, the Ottawa would send out scouts in the night to reconnoiter the enemy's camp and gauge his strength in men and arms. The scouts would then report back to the war party, which would gather in council to consider the next step. Although Indians were sometimes characterized by whites as impulsive fighters who attacked without thinking, Cadillac observed that the Ottawa weighed the chances of success carefully before taking on the enemy—a cautiousness that was shared by the war leaders of most other tribes, who hesitated to expend precious lives in a futile bid for glory. If the Ottawa judged that they were strong enough to prevail, however, they wasted no time in acting. "They go at once," Cadillac noted, "generally by night, with the scouts at their head, who never lose their impression of the way they went nor of the encampment of their enemies. When they get within a certain distance, they throw themselves flat on the ground, always keeping a lookout with eyes and ears, and having scouts in front and rear and on both flanks. In this posture they wait daybreak, as that is the time when a man is heaviest from the inclination and longing for sleep, and also that they may be able to see better when they make their onslaught and take advantage of the remainder of the day for making their retreat.

"Their custom is to drag themselves along on the ground on all fours like cats and approach within pistol shot; they then rise to their full height before shooting. The chief of the party gives his signal by a low cry. The others immediately give a loud whoop, and if they have guns, they fire all together at the enemy; if not, they let fly their arrows. After their first volley, if they see that the enemy is thrown into disorder and routed, they rush upon them, hatchet or tomahawk in hand; if they are victorious, they take the scalps of those who are killed. If they capture any prisoners, they bind them and pinion them so tightly that the bonds cut into their flesh; then they travel night and day until they are out of danger and are safe from their enemies."

This surreptitious way of fighting—with its silent approach, lightning assault, and rapid withdrawal—was favored by Indians all across the continent. Although some of the maneuvers described by Cadillac were specific to the eastern woodlands, the urge to surprise the foe and make off swiftly with captives or other prizes was common to war parties everywhere, whether they were stealing up on an enemy camp in the Plains,

Covered by the musket fire of white soldiers commanded by French explorer Samuel de Champlain, a force of Huron, Algonquian, and Montagnais Indians storms an Iroquois fort on the banks of Canada's Richelieu River. While fancifully depicting the Indians as naked, this contemporary engraving of the 1610 engagement accurately shows them practicing a European technique of massed attack learned from their French allies.

waiting in ambush for a rival band along a boulder-strewn pass in the Rockies, or paddling across a Pacific harbor by night to storm a village on the Northwest Coast. Such covert tactics were derived in large part from hunting—and like most prudent hunters, native warriors generally limited their take, claiming captives, scalps, and other trophies without devastating the groups they preyed on. As Indians learned to make full use of such European bequests as the horse and the gun, however, they found it easier to reach their enemies and do them lasting damage. So efficient were they at adapting the new resources to their forays that some white soldiers paid them the ultimate compliment of imitating their methods. Yet gains in war-making proficiency carried a steep price for Indian peoples in terms of heightened tribal strife and bloodshed at the very time whites were encroaching upon their territory and challenging their traditions.

The first colonists from Europe who settled in the eastern woodlands in the 16th and 17th centuries were perplexed by the Indian style of fighting, which many of the newcomers thought devious and chaotic. On the one hand, warriors were faulted for skulking about in the woods and attacking their enemies without warning. On the other hand, they seldom did enough damage to their foes to achieve what Europeans deemed a worthwhile victory. Captain John Underhill of the Massachusetts Bay Colony contended that tribes in New England seemed to fight "more for pastime than to conquer and subdue enemies," adding that "they might fight seven years and not kill seven men." In fact, more warriors than that were sometimes killed in a single Indian battle. But it remained to the colonists to introduce the native peoples of New England to the concept of wholesale slaughter. In 1637 Underhill and his fellow soldiers from Massachusetts did just that when they prevailed on their Indian allies to join them in a merciless assault on a fortified Pequot settlement in Connecticut that claimed the lives of several hundred Pequots in a matter of hours. Appalled by the toll, one of the colonists' Indian allies protested that the attack was for naught, because it was "too furious, and slays too many men."

Destruction on this scale was alien to the native tradition for a number of reasons. Most Indian communities were small and could ill afford to lose the services of many able-bodied men; so offensive expeditions were limited in size and duration, and the leaders who organized them tried to inflict due punishment on the enemy without taking grave risks. Indeed, war chiefs who became too ambitious in their sorties and suffered more than a few casualties as a result were sometimes stripped of their right to command; the Cherokee, for example, rebuked leaders who lost several men to the enemy during an expedition by divesting them of their war names and other tokens of honor and reducing them to the status of youngsters who had never seen battle. Furthermore, the traditional weaponry of the woodlands lacked the devastating impact of firearms. Arrows, clubs, and hatchets could all be deadly, but they could also be dodged or deflected, meaning that opponents could fight bravely and energetically without great carnage. Indian warriors also derived satisfac-

In a watercolor by English colonist John White, based on the drawing of a French artist who ventured to Florida in the 16th century, a warrior holds one of the long hardwood bows used by tribes east of the Mississippi. By the 1700s, the art of making such bows was in decline as the Indians acquired firearms in increasing numbers.

tion from such related military pursuits as crafting weapons, subsisting on the trail, and tracking the enemy—talents that could earn a man the respect of his peers even if he did not kill or capture a man in battle.

Few activities attendant to war were more exacting than that of making weapons. Some tribes had specialists who produced bows, arrow heads, or clubs, but most fighting men took pride in creating their own tools. Woodlands Indians had an ample supply of hickory, ash, beech, and other hardwoods from which to fashion bows. The typical bow was as tall as its maker if not taller—more than six feet in some cases. From

In this scene observed by John White around 1585, an Algonquian village in North Carolina is fortified by a palisade of wooden poles sunk in the ground. Perhaps using artistic license to show details inside, White drew the poles farther apart than they would normally have been. Such palisades, sometimes reinforced with crossbeams and chinked with clay or mud, were built to present an appearance of impregnability.

front to back, it was thick at the handle for a sure grip, with tapered limbs on either side. The tapering made the bow easier to draw, but sacrificed some of its power. Nevertheless, a hickory bow carried by a native warrior in New England could propel an arrow more than 150 yards, and many of the bows had a killing range of about 100 yards. Bowstrings generally were made from animal sinew, which was first softened by chewing and then twisted for strength.

Every warrior learned to make arrows from an early age. He picked a strip of wood about three feet long and less than one inch thick, scraped off the bark, and straightened the shaft by parching it over hot coals. He then tapered and notched the butt of the arrow to fit the bowstring. To provide stability and accuracy in flight, he split feathers down the spine, trimmed them neatly, and lashed two or three segments to the shaft just in front of the notch. Finally, he armed the front end of the projectile with an arrowhead, which was usually chipped from flint, chert, quartz, or obsidian, although some woodlands Indians crafted points of bone, antler, or native copper. Once the base of the arrowhead was wedged into a slot on the shaft, the point was bound tight with sinew.

Arrows, like bows, were decorated with distinctive markings to identify the owner, for warriors who had put so much time and effort into making the shafts went to considerable lengths to retrieve them. Men on the trail carried three dozen or more arrows in a leather or reed quiver, which they wore over the shoulder, where they could quickly draw another projectile once the first one was in flight. Colonists were duly impressed by both the speed and the strength of Indian bowmen, who could unleash several shots in the time that it took a man to load and fire a musket. Spaniards in the Southeast found that their chain mail offered them little protection against Indian arrows and opted for thick cotton quilting, but their exposed limbs remained vulnerable, as did their mounts. In one instance, a Spanish horse was killed by an arrow that passed clear through its thigh and penetrated the chest cavity. In the Northeast in 1606, a Frenchman who was lying low during an Indian attack was slain by an arrow that first went through his dog, leaving man and animal impaled on the same shaft.

For woodlands Indians, the bow and arrow was the weapon of first resort. Warriors often loosed their arrows when they were still some distance from the enemy, which made them less vulnerable to counterfire but meant that alert opponents could evade the shafts. When rival bowmen challenged each other from afar in a clearing, they typically dodged about between shots in order to present a tougher target. As Roger Williams, founder of the Rhode Island Colony, remarked of such encounters, the warriors were so adept at "leaping and dancing, that seldom an arrow hits." These face-offs sometimes ended inconclusively after each side had exhausted its supply of arrows. But war parties intent on inflicting more serious damage followed up the initial volley by charging their opponents and assailing them with a variety of other weapons in their arsenal. Spears and lances were wielded by only a few prominent warriors, usually as a token of their high status. But nearly every fighting man carried a club of some kind.

Such handy weapons were fashioned in various ways. Some warriors unearthed young hardwood saplings when the trunks were only a few inches thick; the lower section of the trunk served as the handle, while the heavy rootball at the base of the sapling formed the business end of the club. For added effect, the roots might be pruned down and sharpened to form spikes, or the ball might be filed smooth and embedded with one or more menacing stone points. Alternatively, men attached heavy round stones or chiseled blades to wooden shafts and used them to pound their enemies or slash at them.

Early on, woodlands Indians called whatever bludgeoning instrument they made in this fashion a tomahawk—a word derived from the Algonquian language family spoken by Native Americans across much of the East, from Canada to the Carolinas. It was only after European traders made metal hatchets widely available, however, that the term *tomahawk* became associated specifically with axlike weapons. By whatever name, the hand tools of Indian warriors could do serious damage. An all-out blow from a stone club at close range could kill an opponent—or the attacker might exert less force, with the object of stunning his enemy and claiming him as a captive. Some warriors were expert at hurling their tomahawks so that the head struck the target dead-on. Whites who fought with or against Indians reported instances of warriors first wounding opponents with arrows from a distance, then closing in partway to finish their quarry off with a well-aimed cast of the tomahawk. Some witnesses maintained that an Indian thus equipped was a greater threat at 40 yards than one who held a rifle in his hands.

However dramatic, such feats of weaponry were just a small part of the warrior's repertoire of skills. In the dense woodlands, finding the enemy could be as difficult a task as fighting him. War parties sometimes went out for weeks in pursuit of the foe—expeditions that required the participants to negotiate obstacles such as rivers and swamps, survive on whatever food they could carry or catch along the way, travel undetected for days on end in hostile country, and communicate clearly without betraying their presence to the enemy.

During warm weather, when most of the war expeditions took place, the uniform worn by the typical southeastern brave consisted of little more than a breechcloth and a pair of moccasins, which offered sufficient protection for the warrior's tough feet while allowing him to move quietly through the forest; among the few items that the men brought with them on the warpath were leather and cord to repair their moccasins. The enduring legend that the woodlands Indians could stalk their prey in the forest without so much as breaking a twig was not entirely without foundation. Among some tribes, men on the trail who snapped a fallen branch underfoot were required to carry the broken pieces with them as a token of their clumsiness. In the Northeast, where war parties occasionally went out to surprise their enemies in the late fall or winter, men donned snowshoes for speed and stealth.

In many parts of the woodlands, but particularly in the northern lakes region, warriors pursued their enemies—and sometimes clashed with them—in birch-bark canoes that were light enough to be portaged between bodies of water. Cadillac observed that the canoes belonging to Ottawa warriors were painted various colors and decorated with symbols of guiding spirits such as the raven or the bear. When a war party departed from the village, he added, men poised in their canoes would "give a great shout all together and start off at the same moment in the direction in which they are to go, as if they saw the enemy before them, and it may be said that their boats are like arrows." Some of the tribes that lived in the vicinity of large lakes or bays fashioned heavier war canoes by hollowing out long tree trunks. Vessels such as these could carry from 20 to 50 men and withstand a moderate swell.

Since most warriors were also skilled hunters, they usually had little trouble obtaining food while they were on their way to hostile territory. But once they were within range of the enemy, they risked betraying themselves if they chased after game or kindled fires. In order to avoid detection, woodlands warriors carried dry rations—usually cornmeal, which could be mixed with cold water and consumed as gruel. With such "ready provision, and their bows and arrows," Roger Williams noted, Rhode Island Indians were prepared to take to the warpath "at an hour's warning." It was no accident that groups such as the Iroquois who har-

A painted birch-bark model of an Ottawa war canoe sports the high prow and stern favored by Great Lakes tribes. Made in 1820 by Ottawa chief Jean-Baptiste Assiginack, the three-foot-long vessel carries six wooden figures representing actual Ottawa tribesmen.

In a territorial dispute of the sort that became common as European incursions raised tribal tensions, Ojibwa and Mesquakie Indians clash on Lake Superior in the mid-1600s. By 1670 the Ojibwa had driven the Mesquakie south, claiming the shores of Superior as their own.

vested corn in abundance were also known to mount large and lengthy war expeditions.

Communicating without alerting the foe was a thorny problem for warriors living in the woodlands. Hand signals or other visual cues were of little value for scouts operating at night or warriors groping toward an enemy camp through dense foliage at dawn. One solution to the dilemma was to communicate through animal calls—a skill some Native Americans refined to the point that their mimicry was all but indistinguishable from the real thing. Cherokee war parties sent out four scouts, each identified by the animal whose call he would sound if he spotted the enemy. The chief of the war party—designated the Raven— ranged up front. To his left and right lurked the Wolf and the Owl, while the Fox trotted behind. In such deadly games, the hunters could easily become the hunted, and war parties used every trick they knew to throw enemies off the scent. Chickasaw scouts sometimes attached bear paws to their feet in order to confound their enemy counterparts.

Tribes who feared retribution from their foes did not wait passively for the blow to fall. In addition to sending out their own scouts to warn of an impending attack, their leaders sometimes divided a vulnerable community into several mobile bands and dispersed them, or drew people together within one of the many fortified villages that dotted the woodlands. Some eastern Indians lived permanently inside such stockades, while others took refuge there only when an attack appeared imminent. These sanctuaries, which might be either oval or rectangular, were girded by palisades consisting of tree trunks set deep in the ground and rising to a height of 10 feet or more.

Prudent chiefs kept such forts stocked at all times with food and water to resist long sieges, and few attackers tried to storm their narrow entrances, which were obstructed by brush or other materials and guarded by well-armed defenders. Although warriors laying a siege had the capacity to set fire to the buildings within the stockade by shooting flaming arrows over the palisade, such stratagems were generally frowned upon. Instead, the attackers usually tried to lure their opponents from the stock-

A 17th-century musketeer carries the accouterments that made firing a matchlock musket a cumbersome process unsuited to swift and stealthy Indian warfare. The heavy barrel rested on a forked staff, and a smoldering cord ignited the gun's priming powder.

ade by hurling insults. If several of the defenders responded and were killed or captured outside the palisade, the attackers were normally satisfied and ended the siege, heading home with their scalps or prisoners.

This traditional pattern of chronic but limited conflict in the woodlands began to change in the 17th century as Indians there obtained firearms, a development that coincided with other destabilizing events such as the spread of European-borne diseases and competition among tribes for white trade goods. Although most Indians were horrified by their first exposure to firearms—"thunder weapons," some called them—they soon mastered their fear. Many an Indian turned out to be a better shot than the typical colonist.

Few white settlers of the day were noted for their marksmanship. Hunting was an upper-class pastime in Europe, and even among the privileged, bringing down animals with a gun was considered vaguely unsporting. John Winthrop, governor of the Massachusetts Bay Colony, echoed the prevailing sentiment when he remarked that hunting with a musket "brings a man of worth and godliness into some contempt." To be sure, some Europeans who sailed for the New World had been drilled to fire guns in battle, but the object of such training was to teach recruits to deliver a hail of fire at enemy ranks, not to hit a discrete target. Furthermore, most of the muskets that the earliest settlers carried to America were troublesome pieces known as matchlocks, which weighed up to 20 pounds, sometimes had to be propped on a rest before firing, and required that the soldier light the match—a slow-burning cord that ignited the powder—and keep it burning come rain or shine.

The matchlock was soon supplanted in the colonies by the flintlock, a lighter musket that did not require a prop, was far easier to load, and provided its own igniting spark from a flint attached to the hammer. Indians were quick to recognize the advantages of flintlocks and did all they could to obtain them. William Bradford, governor of the Plymouth Colony, reported that when the surrounding Wampanoag Indians saw what the colonists' guns could do, "they became mad (as it were) after them and would not stick to give any price they could attain to for them, accounting their bows and arrows but baubles in comparison." As a result, such trade flourished, even though selling guns to the native peoples carried heavy penalties in many colonies. Traffic in guns was especially rampant in the Northeast, where the Dutch, French, and English maneuvered for

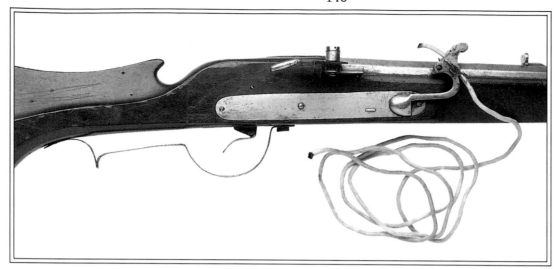

The firing mechanism of an early-17th-century matchlock musket consists of the twisted cord match and a priming pan containing powder. A pull of the trigger brought the smoldering match down to ignite the priming powder and set off the charge.

Flintlocks, like this one from the 1700s, were the technological successors to matchlocks, and more reliable and handier in battle for both Indian and white man. When the trigger was pulled, a piece of flint struck a spark that instantly ignited the powder.

advantage by selling firearms to Indians hostile to their rivals. Despairing of keeping muskets out of the hands of the Indians, Governor Bradford could only lament in verse: "Thus like madmen we put them in a way, With our own weapons us to kill and slay."

Even before Indians in the region came to rely significantly on firearms in battle, they were using flintlocks to hunt game, both for their own consumption and for trade with whites who lacked their tracking skills. With keen eyes and quick reflexes honed by hunting with the bow, Indians became adept at shooting deer, waterfowl, and other game. Several colonies placed bounties on wolves to protect their livestock, and Indian marksmen collected many of the rewards, often accepting payment in the form of powder and shot for their muskets.

For all their facility with firearms, Indians remained wholly dependent on whites for powder and knew little of the art of maintaining a musket. Although a few tribes had smiths of their own who had trained as apprentices with whites and could repair guns, the average musket in Indian hands had a short life—perhaps a few years at best. As a result, Indians were always hungry for more firearms, and competition for guns became an added source of tension between tribes. Along with muskets, Indians obtained other European arms and materials, including sturdy metal points and blades to replace their traditional stone arrowheads and ax heads. New Englander Daniel Gookin reported that by the mid-17th century, tribes of the region had secured not only flintlocks from the Europeans but "pistols, swords, rapier blades fastened unto a staff of the length of a half-pike, hatchets, and axes."

This burgeoning arsenal—and the flood of firearms in particular—altered the course of tribal conflict. A dramatic instance occurred in 1669, when a war party of some 700 Indians led by the Massachusett chief Chekatabutt entered the territory of the rival Mohawk, the easternmost of the five Iroquois tribes. Both sides had guns, but Chekatabutt squandered his ammunition by directing much of it against Mohawks holed up in a sturdy log fort. When Chekatabutt withdrew, Mohawks armed with muskets ambushed his men as they trailed through a tangled swamp, firing on them from dense brush alongside the path. The Massachusett losses were staggering by Indian standards. As Gookin noted: "About 50 of their chief men, they confess, were slain in this fight, but I suppose more."

Here, as in earlier assaults by the Iroquois that devastated their bitter rivals the Huron, the attackers combined the old surprise tactics with the new weaponry to stunning effect. Success on this scale could bring the victors more than retribution. It offered them a chance to reduce their enemies to subject status, or even to absorb them. Consequently, well-armed and well-organized groups such as the Iroquois began to think of warfare in strategic terms—as a way to impose their will permanently on entire populations—a development of far-reaching consequence for tribes in the woodlands and the Plains beyond.

Whites, too, felt the impact of the changes in Native American warfare that their own technology had helped bring about. When Indians led by a Wampanoag chief the English called King Philip rose up against the New England colonists in 1675, settlers had to contend with opponents whose traditional hit-and-run tactics had been significantly enhanced by firepower. The colonists eventually put down the uprising, but not before they learned to appreciate and apply some of the stealthy maneuvers of their foes, including using friendly Indians as scouts, laying traps and ambushes, and firing muskets from cover when possible instead of relying exclusively on their traditional frontal assaults.

Colonists had previously derided such stratagems, likening them to the ruses of wild animals. "We may as well go to war with wolves and bears," complained one settler in the Carolinas, while another colonist questioned the manhood of Indian warriors when he declared that they "durst not look an Englishman in the face in the open field." In the aftermath of King Philip's War, however, more than a few settlers began to recognize that fighting in the woodlands required a certain amount of guile. As one New Englander put it, "God pleased to show us the vanity of our military skill, in managing our arms after the European mode. Now we are glad to learn the skulking way of war."

Lessons learned from the Indians did not alter the fundamentals of combat as practiced by Anglo-Americans, however. As late as the Civil War, soldiers were still being drilled to maneuver in the open field, face their enemy in a rank, and unleash a solid curtain of fire. Such tactics persisted because they were crudely effective, given the limited accuracy of muskets and the punishing objectives of most campaigns, which aimed at crippling large armies, seizing territory, and depriving the enemy of the will and the means to fight. Nonetheless, by late colonial times, shrewd commanders were resorting when appropriate to the "skulking way of war" by regularly deploying scouts to watch for an ambush—or the chance to spring one—staging furtive raids behind enemy lines, and encouraging troops under duress to fire from cover rather than stand and be slaughtered.

In the 18th century, colonial powers vying for control of the eastern woodlands sought to profit from the proven military skills of Indians by recruiting them to fight the white man's battles in exchange for prized goods such as firearms or diplomatic considerations. More than once, Indians played a prominent role in such campaigns. On one notorious occasion, in 1755, the British general Edward Braddock led a combined force of 1,500 British regulars and colonial militiamen against hostile French forces and their Indian allies holding Fort Duquesne, at the site of present-day Pittsburgh.

Tukosee Mathla, a Seminole chief whose portrait was painted in 1826, holds an English trade musket, the lightweight flintlock prized by the Indians. English traders sold the gun throughout North America until the middle of the 19th century.

Approaching that stronghold along a forest trail, Braddock's vanguard collided with a small number of French and Canadian troops accompanied by several hundred Indians. The surprised British got off a thundering volley, but the Indians— watched over by their own war leaders—maintained their composure and fanned out with some of the French forces into the woods on either side of the clearing, where they poured lead into Braddock's exposed column.

Sketched on the Yukon River in 1847, a Kutchin Indian shoulders his buckskin-encased trade musket. In the north, guns came with red woolen covers. When the cloth wore out, the Indians stitched up buckskin sheaths.

Among those soldiers facing fire in the clearing were Virginia militiamen under the command of George Washington. The Virginians knew something about fighting Indians in the forest, and they scurried to the edge of the woods, where they took cover behind fallen timbers and began trading shots with their opponents. Braddock shouted at them to maintain ranks "and fight like men, not animals." But not all of the Virginians heeded his orders. Soon, even some of his redcoats were seeking cover, and Braddock had to brandish his sword in an effort to keep them in line. Gripped by panic, the British never properly deployed, and their fitful fire did more harm to the friendly Virginians than to the Indians and French. Before long, Braddock's beleaguered men were huddled in knots in the clearing, where a single bullet sometimes claimed two or three victims. Braddock himself was fatally wounded, and the survivors fell back in disarray, leaving nearly 1,000 men dead or captured. Following this crushing defeat, Benjamin Franklin declared that conventional maneuvers had been shown "by experience to be of little or no use in our woods." British general John Forbes went even further, asserting that now whites "must comply and learn the art of war from enemy Indians."

Elsewhere in North America, the tactical interchange between Europeans and Indians assumed a different character. In the Pacific Northwest, for example, where merchant ships began visiting the coast in the 18th century, Indians eagerly traded for flintlocks, but they found that the muskets often misfired in the damp climate and were not easily adapted to the covert raids most war leaders favored over pitched battles. Men stealing up on a village to wreak vengeance and claim captives, for example, often tried to elude detection and creep right into the houses of their sleeping prey before pouncing—a maneuver that was best carried out with traditional weapons such as clubs and knives. Whites, for their part, learned that their guns offered them no proof against attacks by tribes they antagonized. More than once, Indians armed only with clubs, axes, or bows overwhelmed European crews before they could bring their muskets to bear.

The impact of firearms was also blunted somewhat by the sturdy defenses employed by many coastal tribes. The armor long worn there by warriors to fend off traditional weapons—typically consisting of a heavy wooden helmet and a thick hide shirt, often covered by a breastplate of wooden slats—was substantial enough to offer some protection against musket balls fired at a distance, although the use of armor declined as Indians acquired more guns and deployed them to greater effect. Of more importance, many coastal tribes, like their counterparts in the eastern woodlands, took refuge in times of stress in stout log fortifications situated on islands or other remote spots—strongholds that were not easily stormed, even by men with muskets. To be sure, tribes that secured large numbers of guns before their rivals did were better equipped to overwhelm opposing warriors and capture their women and children, but such punishing assaults on the populace were a fact of life in the Pacific Northwest long before the introduction of firearms.

In a few other regions, contact between whites and Indians was so slight as to have negligible effect on the conduct of native warfare. Nowhere was this more evident than in the Colorado River basin, where the Quechan occupying the lower reaches of that river clashed or trafficked sporadically with Spanish intruders from the 17th century on, but borrowed so little from them in terms of weapons or tactics that the tribe's climactic battle with the Maricopa and Pima in 1857 was fought in thoroughly traditional fashion. The situation was far different across the vast grasslands of the North American interior. There, the ways of Indian warriors changed dramatically once white men had introduced the two great catalysts—horses and firearms.

Prior to the time that those innovations took hold, Indian war parties on the Plains were limited in their range and destructive effect. The bow they carried was long, similar to the one used in the woodlands, and its wooden stave was typically backed with a lining of resilient buffalo sinew that made the weapon even more powerful than its eastern counterpart. Such reinforced bows would have been devastating at short range, but in combat, the early bowmen of the Plains may have deliberately held off

ARMOR OF THE PACIFIC PEOPLES

In the Pacific Northwest, where war parties sometimes clashed head-on in fierce melees, Indian fighting men were renowned for their sturdy armor. A Tlingit warrior entered battle wearing a wooden helmet so heavy it felt "as if it had been made of iron," according to a Spaniard who tried one on in 1791. In addition, men derived protection from thick hide tunics, snug breastplates of slats or rods, and stout wooden shields. This gear served well against arrows and clubs but proved less effective against firearms. By the late 19th century, such majestic armor was used largely for ceremonial purposes.

Girded for war in a sheath of wooden rods and a fur-covered helmet, an archer from the Karok tribe of northern California draws his bow. Clutched beneath his arm is an animal skin quiver.

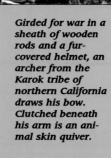

Wooden rods were lashed together with cords of sinew to form this breastplate, worn by an Aleut islander before Europeans arrived in the Aleutians.

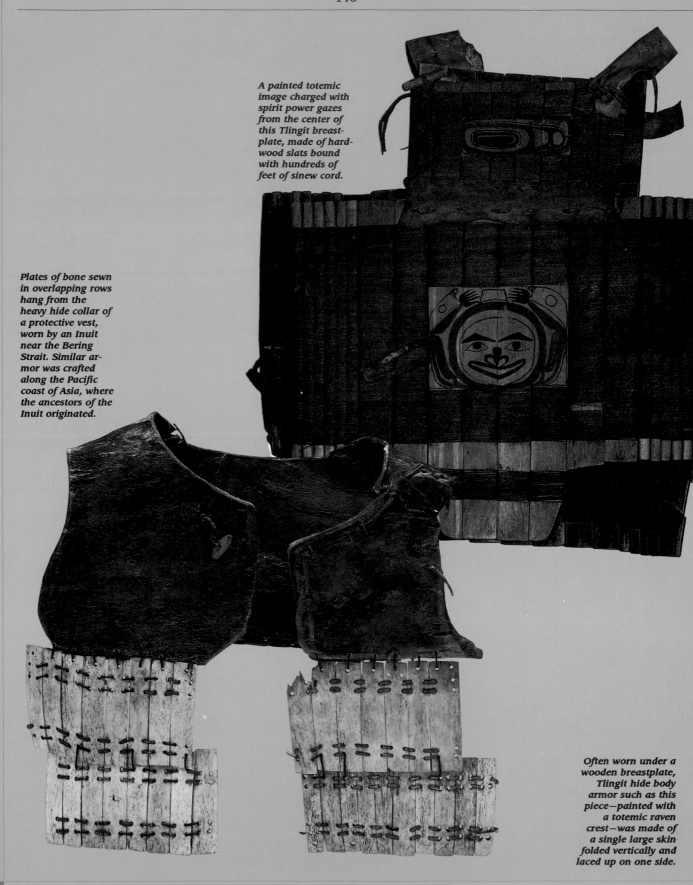

A painted totemic image charged with spirit power gazes from the center of this Tlingit breastplate, made of hardwood slats bound with hundreds of feet of sinew cord.

Plates of bone sewn in overlapping rows hang from the heavy hide collar of a protective vest, worn by an Inuit near the Bering Strait. Similar armor was crafted along the Pacific coast of Asia, where the ancestors of the Inuit originated.

Often worn under a wooden breastplate, Tlingit hide body armor such as this piece—painted with a totemic raven crest—was made of a single large skin folded vertically and laced up on one side.

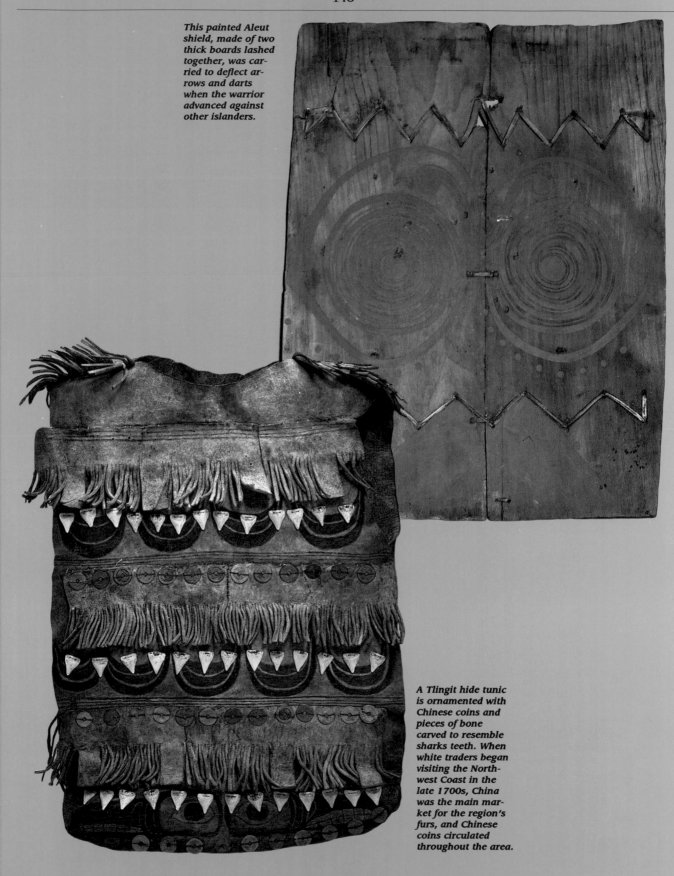

This painted Aleut shield, made of two thick boards lashed together, was carried to deflect arrows and darts when the warrior advanced against other islanders.

A Tlingit hide tunic is ornamented with Chinese coins and pieces of bone carved to resemble sharks teeth. When white traders began visiting the Northwest Coast in the late 1700s, China was the main market for the region's furs, and Chinese coins circulated throughout the area.

from their opponents and fired long shots that tended to be more impressive than lethal. A tale that has been passed down by the Blackfeet Indians tells of an old encounter in which rival forces of Blackfeet and Shoshone warriors, carrying bows and large shields, approached each other on foot and formed battle lines some distance apart. The opposing bowmen proceeded to launch arcing shots from behind their shields, to little effect. When darkness fell, the skirmish concluded indecisively, without a single man killed on either side.

The pace of intertribal conflict began to increase on the Plains around 1700 as horses spread north from Spanish colonies in Mexico and the Southwest, and firearms filtered west from the woodlands along with displaced tribes. Just as the horse changed the subsistence patterns of Plains peoples—some of whom ceased to be planters and became hunters instead—so too did it revolutionize their concept of warfare. Now they could make deep, swift raids into hostile territory, pillage villages and steal horses or other animals, and make off as quickly as they had come. In most instances, Plains warriors dismounted once they reached their target, but they still needed weapons that could be easily carried on horseback and deployed from the mount, if the occasion arose. As a result, bows grew smaller—as short as two and a half feet in some cases. A few western tribes discovered that they could craft good compact bows from the horns of elk or bighorn sheep.

Although the smaller bows packed less power, warriors compensated by using them at closer range and firing faster. Claims of such skills were sometimes exaggerated, but Cheyenne braves were said to be able to unleash six arrows in such rapid order that all would be in flight before the first shot struck its mark. Bowmen practiced hitting moving targets by aiming at a rolling hoop or a moccasin tossed in the air while they themselves were on the run. And because enemies on open ground could still find cover behind a boulder or a dead horse, men trained for that contingency by shooting their arrows in gentle arcs at stationary targets. Some tribes made their arrows even deadlier by coating the tips with poison. The Western Apache, for example, concocted a potent toxin by grinding up a deer's spleen, mixing in various roots and plants, and storing the blend in a bag made from the animal's intestine. "When all is ready," one warrior recollected, "the maker spits into the bag and ties it up tightly and quickly so that none of the bad air will escape. The bag is hung from a tree for about three to five days till good and rotten and in liquid form." This ripe poison was then painted on the arrowheads.

Even as bows grew shorter in order to suit the requirements of mounted warfare, the bulky shield of earlier times was reduced to a disk of rawhide stretched over a wooden frame that was just big enough to cover the warrior's upper torso. Men carried the disks in front of them during an attack and then slung them over their backs when retreating. Since the shield and the designs painted on it were invested with mystic power, its loss was a grievous blow to a man's spirit. When one Kiowa brave lost his shield, he had to do penance by putting aside his bow and relying instead on a lance. Although lances and spears encumbered Plains warriors, they served well for stabbing opponents during a charge and were often adorned with feathers or scalps that proclaimed a man's exploits and lent him courage. Mounted men sometimes carried clubs as well, but heavy tomahawks of the sort wielded by eastern warriors were largely ceremonial in the West.

As was the case with their eastern counterparts, Plains peoples at first dreaded the noise, fire, and smoke of the musket but soon fathomed its mysteries and became devoted to it. "Medicine iron," the Sioux called the gun, and such was its allure that braves were soon trading horses for muskets, one for one. Most purchases were made by individuals rather than tribes, so there was considerable diversity in the selection of models. But in firearms as in traditional weapons, mounted warriors looked for designs that were light and easily wielded in battle.

Muskets first reached the Plains Indians through the hands of white fur traders in the Great Lakes region. Several trading outfits, including one called the North West Company, distributed a class of musket that proved especially popular. Known collectively as North West trade guns, they had barrels averaging about three feet in length—shorter than most muskets of the day. Many Indians trimmed the weapon further by filing several inches off the barrel to make the gun handier on horseback. One white man traveling among the Blackfeet in the mid-19th century remarked that after pruning, the barrel on such muskets emerged "little longer than that of a horse pistol." The discarded metal was often used to form useful articles such as scrapers for cleaning buffalo hides.

As white traders fanned out across the Plains, they offered these muskets in exchange for buffalo hides or, preferably, sleeker and more valuable furs such as fox pelts. During the 1850s, agents of the Hudson Bay Company were trading their version of the North West gun to the Cree on the northern Plains for three silver fox pelts or five buffalo hides. Indians who had ready access to the traders would then exchange their

The scarcity of suitable wood forced some Plains and Plateau bow makers to craft their weapons of alternative materials. This early-19th-century Mandan bow is a composite in which the inner curve, or belly, is made of horn or antler, and the outer curve of rawhide or sinew.

Dramatically silhouetted in a 1913 photograph, a Crow archer takes aim with a short bow of the type employed to devastating effect by Plains horsemen during the 18th and 19th centuries. Mounted warfare demanded a shorter, handier weapon than the long bow that was common on the Plains prior to the advent of the horse.

surplus guns with distant tribes, customarily asking horses in return. Some manufacturers attempted to take advantage of the eager Indian market by producing shoddy replicas of the North West gun, but the native customers were quick to reject the inferior models. In one instance, an arms maker abandoned the sound practice of fashioning the gunstock out of a single piece of wood and instead joined two shorter pieces together at the breech. "This the Indians cannot endure," an agent with the American Fur Company complained in writing to his purchasing office in 1832. "When the stock is new and varnished, you hardly discover this imperfection," he noted. But once the guns were used or exposed to the weather, he added, the flaw was readily apparent: "Very often the Indians bring them back to be exchanged for better, or those who have them on credit will not pay for them."

Even the better trade guns had distinct drawbacks. Their accuracy was limited to start with, and shortening the barrel decreased the range at which they could be fired effectively. This was not considered a prohibitive defect, however, since Plains Indians—like their woodlands counterparts—tended to dodge back and forth when they were fighting in the open, making it difficult for a man to take dead aim on his opponent even with the surest of weapons. A greater inconvenience from the warrior's point of view was the time and trouble it took to recharge the muzzleloading muskets with powder, ram the ball home, and fire—an operation that consumed up to 30 seconds. On one occasion, a white trader and his Indian companion thwarted an attack by Blackfeet warriors on Fort Benton in present-day Montana by shooting down five of the raiders while they were straining to reload their muskets.

Mindful of such risks, some mounted warriors preferred to trust exclusively in the bow and arrow. But other braves sought faster ways to reload. One trick was to carry spare lead balls in one's mouth while riding and spit them down the barrel on top of a powder charge. The bullets had to be of a smaller caliber than the bore, and the loose shots often went awry, but the shortcut allowed the warrior to dispense with a ramrod and get off four or five rounds in the space of a minute.

No weapon in his arsenal was more important to the fighting man on the Plains than a good horse. Even warriors who dismounted before a raid or ambush depended mightily on their best horse to speed them beyond the reach of pursuers afterward. Men who fought on horseback brought along two mounts if they could, one swift and sturdy animal for the trail and an even quicker one for the actual engagement. From this war-horse, the brave derived much of his confidence. "An Indian mounted on an animal which he considers better than that of his enemies does not fear to penetrate into their very midst," observed a westerner named William Clark. The Plains warrior sometimes signaled his spiritual bond to his horse by painting the animal in the same pattern as he did his own body before entering battle.

Hard-riding warrior bands such as the Comanche, who often fought from horseback, appeared more at home astride their animals than they did on solid ground. "The Comanches are in stature rather low, and in person often approaching to corpulency," remarked artist George Catlin during a journey across the southern Plains in the 1830s. "In their movements they are heavy and ungraceful," he added, "but the moment they mount their horses, they seem at once metamorphosed, and surprise the spectator with the ease and elegance of their movements."

Such facility was the product of rigorous training that began when a youngster was four or five and mounted his first colt. As the boy grew taller and stronger, he would mind his family's herd and ride in horse

The feathers and decorated tack on the horses of this Oglala Sioux war party reflect the high esteem in which Indians held their mounts. Viewed as extensions of their riders, war-horses entered into battle painted and dressed in full warrior regalia.

Courageous war-horses were revered by their owners, who sang the praises of their steeds in victory ceremonies and carved wooden effigies like this one to honor mounts killed in battle. The red-painted holes represent the bullet wounds of the slain Sioux pony.

races, competing to the cheers of his neighbors and kin, who gambled on the outcome. In time, he honed his reflexes for combat by plucking objects from the ground at the gallop. To evade hostile fire, he practiced hooking one leg over the horse's back while concealing the rest of his body along the animal's flank and shooting arrows from beneath its neck.

These feats were accomplished with the simplest of gear. Most Plains warriors did without saddle and stirrups, riding on a blanket or a pad stuffed with buffalo hair and guiding the horse with a single rein attached to a rope looped around the mount's lower jaw. Since the rider's hands might be occupied with his bow or gun during battle, he also trained the animal to obey voice commands or pressure from the knees and heels. The ability of the warrior to manage his horse while wielding weapons appeared to Catlin "to be the result of magic," but in fact such wizardry was achieved only through years of practice and conditioning.

While the tricks of fighting on horseback were mastered by relatively few tribes, most Plains warriors were adept at surviving on the trail, tracking the enemy, and communicating through signals. White men new to the Plains often found the landscape bewilderingly monotonous, but natives of the region knew how to read the terrain and distinguish its subtle variations. Where nature offered no clear signposts, Indians created their own by piling up rocks in mounds that dot the Plains to this day. Seasoned fighting men retained a mental map of the trails they had followed and shared that intelligence with the inexperienced warriors before starting out. Among the Comanche, veteran war leaders would chart the expedition in advance for the assembled party, laying sticks on the ground to mark off each day and describing in detail the landmarks that would be encountered along the way. Such meticulous planning by the Comanche and others meant that the people left behind in the village or camp sometimes knew to the day when the warriors expected to reach their objective and when they planned to return.

The warrior's first concern on the trail was to elude detection in a setting that offered long vistas and little cover. In rolling country, the leader and his followers would stay low, avoiding the crests of hills; on flat expanses, men would sometimes drape themselves in buffalo hides to deceive enemy scouts. When they reached rivers that were too deep for men or horses to wade across, Mandan and Hidatsa warriors relied on so-called bullboats—small, lightweight vessels made of hide stretched over a wooden frame—while members of other tribes placed their gear on rafts and towed them with ropes strung around the necks of strong swimmers.

War parties on the northwestern Plains took advantage of the wooded areas along rivers or atop hills to build conic lodges that could not be seen from the surrounding country. Framed of timbers covered with overlapping strips of bark, these way stations were usually located within a few days' journey of suspected enemy camps or hunting grounds. Here, warriors who had ventured far from their home base could rest and re-provision while scouts searched for signs of the foe. A few members of the party were dispatched to hunt for buffalo, and the meat they retrieved was dried over a fire made with dry willow or other well-seasoned wood that produced little smoke. Each member of the band would then pack his ration of meat in a rawhide pouch and carry it with him when the scouts brought word of the enemy and the war party moved out.

Among the Blackfeet, women who did not have children to care for frequently accompanied their men to these lodges and sometimes even joined in the ensuing raids. As one warrior recollected: "My wife said she loved me, and if I was to be killed on a war party, she wanted to be killed, too. I took her with me on five parties. Some of them I led, and my wife was not required to perform the cooking or other chores." This stalwart woman carried her own weapon—a six-shooter—and once sneaked up on the enemy with the rest of the war party and made off with a horse and saddle, an ammunition bag, and a war club.

The scouts assigned by war leaders to track the enemy were alert to sundry clues. Sometimes a scout would detect footprints and could deduce from the impression of the moccasin whether the walker was friend or foe. But most Indians afield tried to avoid leaving such traces by walking on hard ground or wearing animal tails or fringes at their heels that obscured their prints on a dusty trail. The hoofs of horses made a deeper impression, however, and were harder to disguise. When a scout was pursuing raiders who had stolen horses from his camp, for example, he could tell by the depth of hoofprints along a trail whether they had been made by stray horses or by horses that were bearing men. In the latter case, the scout would follow the hoofprints until he came to a place where the riders had dismounted and the tired animals had fallen to the ground, leaving hairs that revealed what color the horses were. This might be sufficient evidence to confirm that the riders were the thieves in question; if the droppings left by the horses were fairly fresh, the scout knew that the culprits were close at hand and would signal for other warriors in his party to take up the chase.

Scouts used various visual cues to send messages to their fellow tribesmen over long distances—an art that was highly developed on the Plains, with its open expanses. Among the systems Indians employed were codes involving puffs of smoke, waves of a blanket, flashes of sunlight reflected in mirrors, gestures made with the arms or with a raised lance, or the maneuvers of men on horseback. A Sioux warrior named Iron Hawk likened these to the forms of communication that Europeans were endowed with: "The whites have had the power given them by the Great Spirit to read and write, and convey information in this way. He gave us the power to talk with our hands and arms, and send information with the mirror, blanket, and pony far away."

Indians who communicated in such fashion needed to possess not only a firm command of the codes but also superb eyesight. Colonel Richard Dodge, who campaigned in the West with the U.S. Army, remarked that the "wonderful thing about this telegraphing is the very great distance at which it can be read by the Indian. I have good 'plains eyes'; but while, even with an excellent field glass, I could scarcely make out that the distant speck was a horseman, the Indian by my side would tell me what the distant speck was saying."

On another occasion, Colonel Dodge watched in awe as a Sioux chief sat on his horse atop a knoll near the South Platte River and flashed orders with a reflecting glass to a force of 100 mounted warriors exercising

Smoke signals could be seen as far as 60 miles away on the treeless reaches of the open Plains, giving warriors a means to communicate over the vast distances that were traversed by mounted war parties.

in the valley below. "For more than half an hour," Dodge observed, "he commanded a drill which for variety and promptness of action could not be equaled by any civilized cavalry of the world." Dodge noted that the warriors regarded the commands as sacred medicine, "the secret of which it would be destruction to divulge." No amount of persuasion or bribery by the colonel could induce the Sioux to betray the code: "They admit the use of the glass, and that is all."

Not all such secrets remained hidden to outsiders, however. Just as white soldiers learned lessons in horsemanship from Plains Indians, they also adopted some of their techniques of long-distance communication. Albert James Myer, an army surgeon serving in the Southwest during the 1850s, observed Comanches sending messages to one another by waving lances and subsequently incorporated elements of their system into the wig-wag flag code he devised for the U.S. Signal Corps. Ironically, Myer first put the flag signals to the test in a campaign waged against Indians in New Mexico.

The native warriors of the West, for their part, were more interested in acquiring the white man's weapons than in adopting his style of warfare, with its punishing frontal assaults. If anything, the introduction of guns to the Plains made Indian chiefs all the more wary of pitched battles. Although warriors were expected to face death without flinching, here, as elsewhere, tribes cherished their young men and leaders risked disgrace if they lost many of their followers to the enemy. As a result, most war parties concentrated on raids or ambushes and met the foe head-on only if circumstances or their sense of honor required it. When set battles did occur, the fighting was often highly individualized, with contests between

the boldest warriors on each side serving in place of a bloody free-for-all. This approach did not necessarily reduce the costs of conflict for the population as a whole, however. Firearms enabled raiders on the Plains to do frightful damage when they descended unannounced on enemy camps or villages—few of which were fortified—and such assaults and the reprisals they spawned often left both sides weaker for the effort.

One such raid was described in detail by an aristocratic German explorer, Prince Maximilian zu Wied, whose journey up the Missouri River in 1833 took him to Fort Mackenzie, a trading post located in present-day Montana. While Maximilian and his party were laying over at the fort, a

A 19th-century hide painting done by a Plains Indian artist portrays a horse raid by warriors equipped with sundry gear, including quirts, bows, lances, and firearms. Stealing horses was regarded as an honorable means for men to prove their mettle. "We took horses from our enemies; it was a challenge in the same way as fighting them," explained a Blackfeet warrior. "They would do exactly the same to us."

A Crow picket pin less than an inch and a half long is a miniature version of the wooden stakes used to tether valuable buffalo and war-horses outside their owners' tipis. This pin was part of a medicine bundle carried to protect a warrior on horse-stealing raids.

band of perhaps 100 Blackfeet men, women, and children were camped nearby. Like other white traders on the Plains, the agents at Fort Mackenzie were in the habit of plying the Indians who visited the post with whiskey in exchange for their furs or other valuables. On the evening of August 27, the Blackfeet stayed up late, drinking and singing around their campfires, before falling asleep. The whiskey may have caused them to let down their guard, for at first light, a force of several hundred Cree and Assiniboin warriors intent on avenging earlier insults by the Blackfeet took the camp by surprise.

Ripping open the tents with knives, the raiders fired on the startled occupants. About a dozen people were killed before the Blackfeet managed to rally and fire back, driving the attackers off long enough for the survivors to retreat with their wounded to the safety of the fort. There, Maximilian and others of his party tried to calm the victims, but the Blackfeet preferred their own spirit-rousing method of treatment. "Instead of suffering the wounded, who were exhausted by the loss of blood, to take some rest," he noted, "their relations continually pulled them about, sounded large bells, and rattled their medicine or amulets."

During the attack, the Blackfeet had dispatched messengers on horseback to their main camp, about 10 miles away, and before long warriors were flocking to the fort to hold off the Crees and Assiniboins, who had regrouped on the brow of a nearby hill. "More and more Blackfeet continued to arrive," Maximilian wrote. "They came galloping in groups, from three to 20 together, their horses covered with foam, and they themselves in their finest apparel, with all kinds of ornaments and arms, bows and quivers on their backs, guns in their hands, furnished with their medicines, with feathers on their heads; some had splendid crowns of black and white eagles' feathers, and a large hood of feathers hanging down behind, sitting on fine panther skins lined with red; the upper part of their bodies partly naked, with a long strip of wolf's skin thrown across the shoulder, and carrying shields adorned with feathers and pieces of coloured cloth."

These men were decked out for war, and the stage appeared to be set for a major battle. But instead, many of the Blackfeet warriors chose to remain in the fort, while the others were content to drive their enemies away from the area and tangle with them now and then when they put up a fight. In the process, the Blackfeet claimed only a few lives, and most of their opponents escaped unharmed. A white trader who aided the Blackfeet that day expressed frustration at their seeming lack of resolve. "Why did they lag behind?" he asked. "Now was the time to show their courage." Yet the Blackfeet were evidently satisfied at holding the enemy at bay and protecting their people in the fort with minimal losses. There would be ample opportunity to strike back at the offending tribes—when they least expected it and could offer little resistance.

This seemingly endless cycle of raiding and retaliation—intensified by tribal displacements and the combined impact of horses and guns—sapped the strength of many Plains peoples over the years, making it harder for them to resist the pressures of white traders, settlers, and soldiers. In the second half of the 19th century, when the U.S. Army launched a series of campaigns aimed at bringing the West under federal control, Indian war parties fought back courageously. But such opposition was hampered by continuing tribal divisions and by the fact that the elusive Indian style of fighting was not easily adapted to the grinding task of confronting enemy troops and annihilating them, whatever the cost. The relentlessness of the army's offensives ultimately demoralized many Indian warriors and their leaders, who regarded the act of fighting as only a small part of their sacred mission and saw no virtue in a brand of warfare that seemed to crush the spirits of victors and vanquished alike. "I am tired; my heart is sick and sad," Chief Joseph of the Nez Percé announced in 1877 after a long and valiant struggle against pursuing army forces. "From where the sun now stands, I will fight no more forever."

The confinement of tribes to reservations did not bring an end to brave deeds and heroic tales. Of the tens of thousands of Native Americans who went to war for the United States in the 20th century, many drew inspiration from stories that had been handed down by their elders—chronicles of the old warriors and their ways. One such account, preserved by the Cheyenne, tells of the trials faced on the warpath by a man known as Plenty Crows, an Arikara Indian who was captured by the Cheyenne as a youngster around 1850 and adopted into the tribe. The raid for which Plenty Crows is remembered was an ill-fated one, but he endured by virtue of his intelligence and fortitude and went on to become a prominent healer, demonstrating that good can be salvaged even from the depths of defeat.

The raid was instigated about 1865 by a Cheyenne named Two Bulls, a member of the Kit Fox Society. Plenty Crows and his close friend, Yellow Hair, belonged to the same society, so it was natural that they should

In a fanciful view of Plains warfare by George Catlin, a mounted Sioux wielding a bow wounds a warrior from the rival Sauk and Mesquakie who has just taken the scalp of another Sioux. Although Catlin's studies of Plains Indian life were drawn mostly from his own observations, this unusual scene was probably based on tales he heard.

be among those summoned to the feast at which Two Bulls called for recruits. The words Two Bulls used on that occasion were not those of an esteemed war leader, acting on the inspiration of a dream or other portent to organize a major expedition. He spoke rather as a restless adventurer, looking for a handful of warriors to join him on a dare. "Friends," Two Bulls said to his guests, "I try to be happy all the time, but today I am more so. I have decided to call for volunteers to go with me against the Shoshone. We will go on foot, and have a chance to take horses and scalps and count coups. We will all have a good time, I know." Nearly all of those present assented, and after a night of singing and feasting, Two Bulls set off with Plenty Crows, Yellow Hair, and nine other warriors for Shoshone territory, along the Wind River in present-day Wyoming.

The raiders proceeded with due caution, sending scouts ahead on either side of the trail to watch for the enemy. After a few days' journey, one of the scouts spotted smoke rising from a Shoshone camp nestled in the Wind River Valley. Under cover of darkness, the Cheyennes descended on their target. As they neared the perimeter of the camp, a cold rain

White ermine pelts hang from this carved, shell-inlaid ceremonial headdress, worn by chiefs of the hard-fighting Tlingit of the Northwest Coast when they laid their animosities to rest in solemn and elaborate peace ceremonies. As the chief danced, loose white eagle or swansdown feathers, signifying honor and peaceful intent, drifted from the crown of the headdress.

began to fall, pelting on the tipis where the Shoshones were taking shelter for the night after tying their best horses to stakes nearby. Stealing a tethered horse was a coup every Cheyenne warrior dreamed of, and the raiders made the most of this opportunity. Plenty Crows and Yellow Hair advanced side by side, passing up the first horses they came to and venturing deep into the camp, where the finest mounts were tied. Claiming one prize each, they led the animals away and rejoined the other raiders, who had met with similar success. In a parting blow to the Shoshones, the Cheyennes separated a number of horses from the main herd outside the camp and slipped off into the night, riding now instead of walking.

As often happened when one tribe raided another, the hunters soon became the hunted. Before dawn, the rain falling on the homeward-bound Cheyennes turned to snow, providing tracks for the Shoshones to follow once they had discovered the theft. Two Bulls paid little heed to the danger, however. After his party had plodded through the snow for a day and a night, he ordered a halt. "I believe we have gotten away," he announced. "Let's rest and build a fire." Plenty Crows disagreed: "My friend, I think you are wrong. I know these Shoshones, and I think right now is the time they may be catching up with us. They never give up when they follow a trail."

Two Bulls remained adamant, however. He branded Plenty Crows a coward and settled down with the others around the fire to await the dawn, leaving it to Plenty Crows and Yellow Hair to double back and watch for the Shoshones. Plenty Crows first got wind of their approach by heeding his horse, which sensed creatures in the distance and grew agitated before Plenty Crows could see anything amiss. Galloping back to the campfire with Yellow Hair, he warned Two Bulls of the impending attack. Once again, the leader chided Plenty Crows for cowardice, but it was Two Bulls who lost his nerve when the Shoshones struck moments later. He raced frantically for the nearest horse—Plenty Crows' own—and hopped on without untying the animal, which started off like a shot and jerked back on its tether, throwing Two Bulls to the ground. It was the last the Cheyennes saw of their reckless leader.

Plenty Crows managed to escape on foot, and later joined Yellow Hair and several other Cheyennes who had eluded the attackers. The survivors were in no mood to celebrate, however. They had only a single horse left, and they were still far from home. Worst of all, Plenty Crows suspected that the Shoshones were waiting for them in ambush farther along the trail. Venturing ahead of the others to confirm his suspicions, he noticed an eagle flying toward the forested crest of a butte. Suddenly, the bird wheeled and flew back in the direction from which it had come. Like the horse the day before, the eagle was telling Plenty Crows that there was danger afoot. He scrambled up the rocky slope, close enough to the crest to spot 50 Shoshones on horseback lurking in the trees.

Plenty Crows tried to alert Yellow Hair and the others in the plain below by signaling with his arms, but the Cheyennes were too far away to read his warning. It was all he could do to save himself by crawling into a crevice. Bursting from cover, the Shoshones swept down on the doomed Cheyennes. Yellow Hair met death boldly, singing the war song of the Kit Fox Society. The last of the Cheyennes left standing was a man named Two Childs, who drew inspiration from the buffalo and wore a tail of the animal in his hair. Both the Cheyenne and the Shoshone would tell of his bravery that day, how he held his ground alone, "roaring like a buffalo bull." The Shoshones fired guns at him, but he refused to go down. Then several men charged him on horseback, but he managed to pull two of them to the ground and stab them, and the rest held back.

Awed by the spirit that possessed him, one Shoshone gestured to Two Childs in sign language, offering him a way out. "Go on home and tell your people what has happened," he signaled. "We will let you go through." But Two Childs simply held out his hands, as if to say, "No, come on and kill me." Finally, the Shoshones all fell on him at once. After they had beaten him to the ground, he was still breathing and struggled to get up, so they finally used their knives to finish him. Then they picked up their dead and departed.

Plenty Crows pulled himself from the crevice and headed home, a haunted man. That night, as he walked alone, he could hear the footsteps of his dead comrades pursuing him. "My friends," he prayed, "have pity on me. I am the only one left. Help me to get home safe, and I will tell your parents and friends what has happened to you." His prayer seemed to appease the restless souls of the dead, and Plenty Crows found the strength to carry on. When he reached camp, he kept faith by telling of his friends and what had befallen them. And the tale survived, for there was wisdom to be gleaned from it. At every recounting, youngsters learned to distinguish the false bravado of Two Bulls from the true courage of Yellow Hair and Two Childs. Above all, they learned to prize the quiet virtues of watchfulness, loyalty, and persistence that had enabled Plenty Crows to travel the Red Road of war without meeting death or dishonor and to resume his rightful journey on the White Road of peace.

THE WEAPONS OF WAR

From the Iroquois of the eastern woodlands to the Kwakiutl of the Pacific Northwest, warriors gained status not only by success in battle but also from their skill in crafting weapons. Boys grew up steeped in the lore of weaponry. Plains youths learned that turkey or buzzard feathers made better arrow fletching than hawk or eagle feathers because the latter were more easily ruined by blood. They knew that chokecherry and ash branches made the best arrow shafts because both could be smoothed and straightened easily. Weapons gained spiritual potency from the divine power of the natural materials from which they were made, as well as from decorative flourishes. A Blackfeet fighter tapped a bear's supernatural might when he attached its jawbone to a metal blade to make a knife. And Indians gave European firearms spirit power when they decorated gunstocks with brass tacks in sacred designs. Some of the weapons on the following pages functioned in ceremony as well as in war. Pipe tomahawks were used as both ritual smoking pipes and lethal fighting tools. And Plains men carried the same embellished lances into battle that they used in war society rituals. Set against a backdrop of early-20th-century photographs, these weapons are a lasting testament to the artistry of devoted warriors.

HIDATSA ARROWS AND CHOKECHERRY WOOD BOW IN TANNED HIDE CASES, C. 1911

BOWS AND ARROWS

**APACHE ARROWS AND RAWHIDE QUIVER,
C. 1880**

**MAIDU ARROWS IN A WILDCAT
SKIN QUIVER**

CROW BOW AND CLOTH CASE DECORATED
WITH BEADS AND HUMAN HAIR

LANCES AND SPEARS

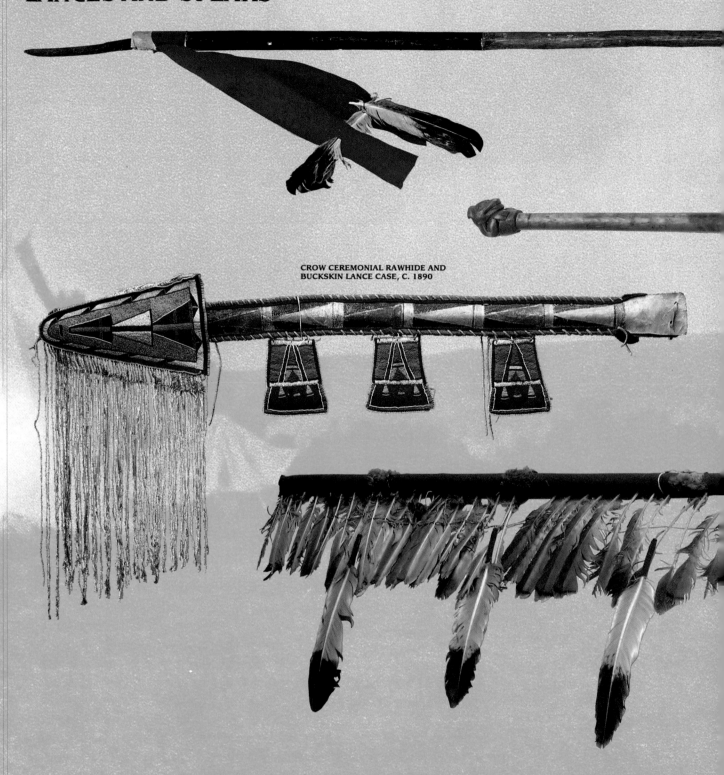

CROW CEREMONIAL RAWHIDE AND
BUCKSKIN LANCE CASE, C. 1890

APACHE WAR LANCE WITH FEATHERS

TLINGIT SPEAR CARVED WITH ANIMAL
GUARDIANS

CHEYENNE DOG SOCIETY LANCE, C. 1904

WAR CLUBS

OSAGE GUNSTOCK CLUB, C. 1820

PLAINS BEADED CLUB

IROQUOIS BALL HEAD CLUB

TSIMSHIAN CEREMONIAL CLUB

TOMAHAWKS

**SIOUX PIPE TOMAHAWK WITH BEADED
AND FRINGED PENDANT**

**WESTERN PLAINS PIPE TOMAHAWK,
STEEL BLADE ON WOODEN HANDLE WITH
BRASS TACK DECORATIONS**

CHICKASAW PIPE TOMAHAWK, C. 1812

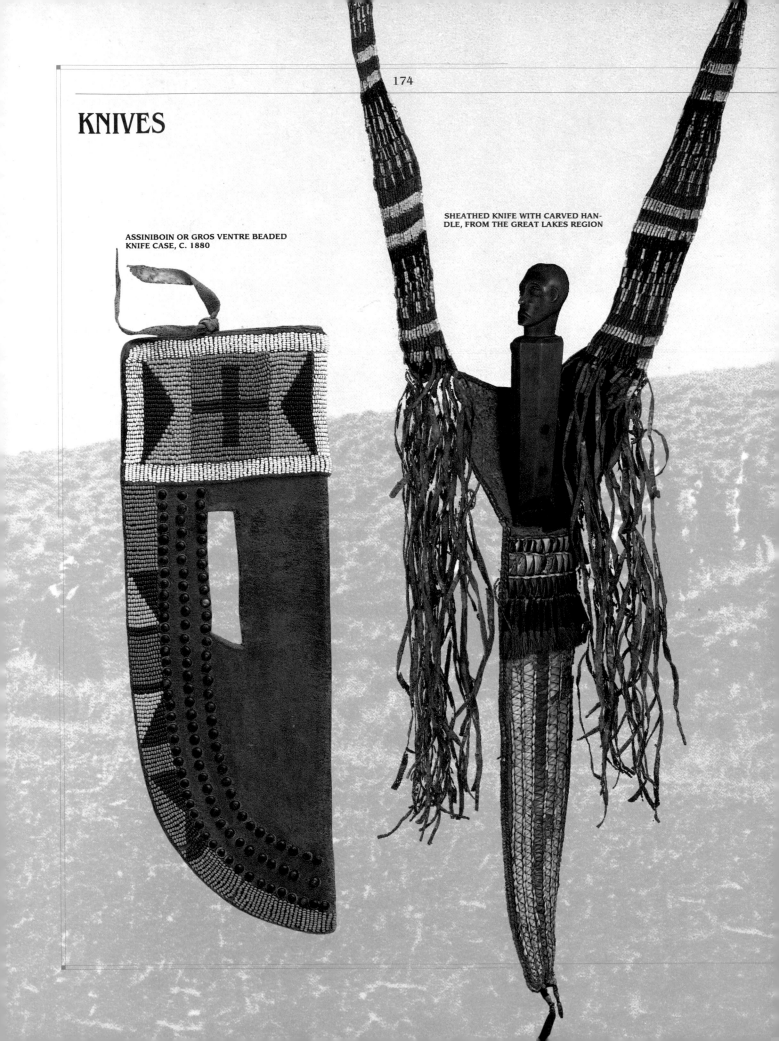

KNIVES

ASSINIBOIN OR GROS VENTRE BEADED KNIFE CASE, C. 1880

SHEATHED KNIFE WITH CARVED HANDLE, FROM THE GREAT LAKES REGION

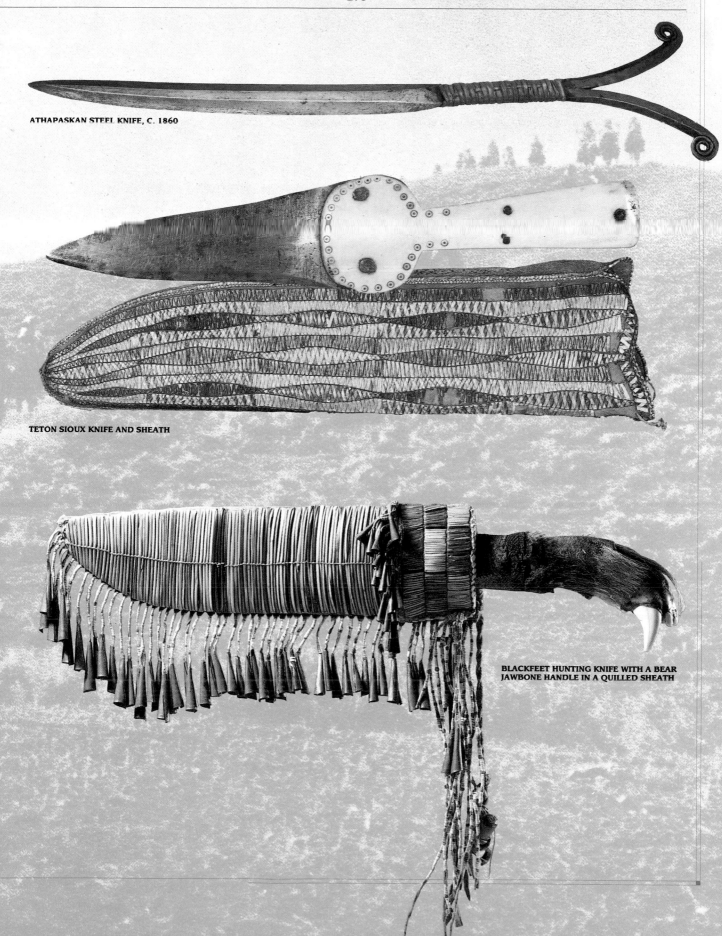

ATHAPASKAN STEEL KNIFE, C. 1860

TETON SIOUX KNIFE AND SHEATH

BLACKFEET HUNTING KNIFE WITH A BEAR
JAWBONE HANDLE IN A QUILLED SHEATH

RIFLES

PENOBSCOT GUNPOWDER HORN INCISED
WITH TRADITIONAL DESIGNS,
18TH CENTURY

BLACKFEET FRINGED AND BEADED BUCK-SKIN GUN CASE, C. 1890

ACKNOWLEDGMENTS

The editors wish to thank the following individuals and institutions for their valuable assistance in the preparation of this volume:

In Canada:
Manitoba—Maureen Dóllenick, Anne Morton, Marie Reidke, Hudson's Bay Company Archives, Provincial Archives of Manitoba, Winnepeg. Ontario—Roanne Moktar, Micheline Robert, National Archives of Canada, Ottawa. Quebec—Chris Kirby, Margery Toner, Canadian Museum of Civilization, Hull.

In France:
Paris—Geneviève Bonté, Conservateur en Chef, Bibliothèque des Arts Décoratifs.

In Germany:
Stuttgart—Ursula Didoni, Axel Schulze-Thulin, Linden-Museum.

In the United States:
Arizona: Flagstaff—George Kirk.
California: Arcata—Erich Schimps, Humboldt State University Library. Fair Oaks—Michael Harrison. Trinidad—Jerome J. Simone, United Indian Health Services.
Colorado: Denver—Cynthia Nakamura, Denver Art Museum.
Illinois: Chicago—Nina Cummings, Field Museum; Harvey Markowitz, D'Arcy McNickle Center for the History of the American Indian, Newberry Library.
Massachusetts: Cambridge—Martha LaBelle, Peabody Museum of Harvard University.
Minnesota: St. Paul—Kay Gutzmann, James Jerome Hill Reference Library; Thomas O'Sullivan, Minnesota Historical Society.
Montana: Billings—Jo Ann Miede, Eastern Montana College Library.

Nebraska: Chadron—Charles Hanson, Jr., Museum of the Fur Trade. Omaha—Marsha Gallagher, Larry Mensching, Joslyn Art Museum.
New York: West Point—David Meschutt, West Point Museum, U.S. Military Academy.
Oklahoma: Anadarko—Vanessa Morgan. Carnegie—Gus Palmer. Durant—Judy Allen, Choctaw Nation.
Rhode Island: Providence—Peter Harrington, Brown University Library.
Washington, D.C.: Donna Nickless, William Truettner, National Museum of American Art, Nicholas J. Parrella, Office of Printing and Photo Services, Smithsonian Institution.
Washington State: Seattle—Rebecca Andrews, Sari Ott, Stan Shockey, University of Washington; Jay Miller.
Wyoming: Cody—Sarah Boehme, Kitty Belle Deernose, Howard Michael Madaus, Buffalo Bill Historical Center.

BIBLIOGRAPHY

BOOKS

Albers, Patricia, and B. Medicine, *The Hidden Half*. Lanham, Md.: University Press of America, 1983.

Axtell, James, *The European and the Indian*. New York: Oxford University Press, 1981.

Baldwin, Gordon C., *The Apache Indians*. New York: Four Winds Press, 1978.

Bancroft-Hunt, Norman, *The Indians of the Great Plains*. London: Orbis Publishing, 1985.

Basso, K. H., ed., *Western Apache Raiding and Warfare*. Tucson: University of Arizona Press, 1971.

Bee, Robert L., *The Yuma*. New York: Chelsea House Publishers, 1989.

Biebuyck, Daniel P., and N. Van den Abbeele, *The Power of Headdresses*. Brussels: Tendi S. A., 1984.

Boas, Franz, *Kwakiutl Ethnography*. Ed. by H. Codere. Chicago: University of Chicago Press, 1966.

Bodmer, Karl, *Karl Bodmer's America*. Omaha: University of Nebraska Press, 1984.

Bowers, Alfred W., *Mandan Social and Ceremonial Organization*. Chicago: University of Chicago Press, 1950.

Broder, Patricia Janis, *Shadows on Glass*. Savage, Md.: Rowman and Littlefield Publishers, 1990.

Bruggmann, Maximilien, and P. R. Gerber, *Indians of the Northwest Coast*. Transl. by B. Fritzemeier. New York: Facts On File Publications, 1989.

Buchanan, Kimberly Moore, *Apache Woman Warriors*. El Paso: Texas Western Press, 1986.

Calloway, Colin G., *The Western Abenakis of Vermont, 1600-1800*. Norman: University of Oklahoma Press, 1990.

Capps, B., and the Editors of Time-Life Books:
The Great Chiefs. (The Old West series). Alexandria, Va.: Time-Life Books, 1985.
The Indians (The Old West series). Alexandria, Va.: Time-Life Books, 1981.

Catlin, George, *Letters and Notes on the Manners, Customs, and Conditions of the North American Indians*. Vols. 1 and 2. New York: Dover Publications, 1973.

Collins, Richard, ed., *The Native Americans*. New York: Smithmark Publishers, 1991.

Conn, Richard, *Circles of the World*. Denver: Denver Art Museum, 1982.

Cooke, David C., *Fighting Indians of America*. New York: Dodd, Mead & Company, 1966.

Cox, Bruce Alden, ed., *Native People, Native Lands*. Ottawa: Carleton University Press, 1988.

Crowe, Rosalie, and S. B. Brinckerhoff, eds., *Early Yuma*. Flagstaff, Ariz.: Northland Press, 1976.

Dempsey, Hugh A., *Crowfoot: Chief of the Blackfeet*. Norman: University of Oklahoma Press, 1972.

Dillon, Richard H., *North American Indian Wars*. New York: Gallery Books, 1983.

Dodge, Richard Irving, *Our Wild Indians*. Freeport, N.Y.: Books for Libraries Press, 1970.

Drimmer, Frederick, ed., *Scalps and Tomahawks*. New York: Coward-McCann, 1961.

Driver, Harold E., *Indians of North America*. Chicago: University of Chicago Press, 1969.

Drucker, Philip, *Cultures of the North Pacific Coast*. San Francisco: Chandler Publishing, 1965.

Dunlay, Thomas W., *Wolves for the Blue Soldiers*. Lincoln: University of Nebraska Press, 1982.

Eckert, Allan W., *Wilderness Empire*. Boston: Little, Brown, 1968.

Erdoes, Richard, *The Sun Dance People*. New York: Random House, 1972.

Erdoes, Richard, and Alfonso Ortiz, eds., *American Indian Myths and Legends*. New York: Pantheon Books, 1984.

Ewers, John C.:
Blackfeet Crafts. Washington, D.C.: United States Department of the Interior, 1945.
The Horse in Blackfoot Indian Culture. Washington, D.C.: Smithsonian Institution Press, 1955.

Ewers, John C., et al., *Views of a Vanishing Frontier*. Omaha: Center for Western Studies and Joslyn Art Museum, 1984.

Fane, Diana, Ira Jacknis, and Lise M. Breen, *Objects of Myth and Memory*. Brooklyn: Brooklyn Museum, 1991.

Farb, Peter, *Man's Rise to Civilization as Shown by the Indians of North America from Primeval Times to the Coming of the Industrial State*. New York: E. P. Dutton, 1968.

Fehrenbach, T. R., *Comanches: The Destruction of a People*. New York: Alfred A. Knopf, 1974.

Fitzhugh, William W., and Aron Crowell, *Crossroads of Continents: Cultures of Siberia and Alaska*. Washington, D.C.: Smithsonian Institution, 1988.

Forbes, Jack D., *Warriors of the Colorado*. Norman: University of Oklahoma Press, 1965.

Gilman, Carolyn, and M. J. Schneider, *The Way to Independence*. St. Paul: Minnesota Historical Society Press, 1987.

Goodwin, Grenville, *The Social Organization of the Western Apache*. Tucson: University of Arizona Press, 1969.

Graybill, Florence Curtis, and Victor Boesen, *Edward Sheriff Curtis: Visions of a Vanishing Race*. Boston: Houghton Mifflin, 1976.

Grinnell, George Bird:
The Cheyenne Indians. Vol. 1. Lincoln: University of Nebraska Press, 1923.
The Fighting Cheyennes. Norman: University of Oklahoma Press, 1956.
Pawnee, Blackfoot and Cheyenne. New York: Charles Scribner's Sons, 1961.

Haines, Francis, *The Plains Indians*. New York: Thomas Y. Crowell, 1976.

Haley, James L., *Apaches: A History and Culture Portrait*. Garden City, N.Y.: Doubleday, 1981.

Hassrick, Royal B., *The Sioux*. Norman: University of Oklahoma Press, 1964.

Heizer, R. F., and M. A. Whipple, eds., *The California Indians*. Berkeley: University of California Press, 1971.

Hodge, Frederick Webb, ed., *Handbook of American Indians North of Mexico*. Parts 1 and 2. New York: Rowman and Littlefield, 1971.

Holm, Bill, *Spirit and Ancestor*. Seattle: University of Washington Press, 1987.

Hook, Jason, *American Indian Warrior Chiefs*. Poole, England: Firebird Books, 1990.

Hoxie, Frederick E., *The Crow*. New York: Chelsea House Publishers, 1989.

Hudson, Charles, *The Southeastern Indians*. Knoxville: University of Tennessee Press, 1976.

Humber, Charles J., ed., *Canada's Native Peoples*. Vol. 2 of *Canada Heirloom Series*. Mississauga, Ontario: Heirloom Publishing, 1988.

Iverson, Peter, ed., *The Plains Indians of the Twentieth Century*. Norman: University of Oklahoma Press, 1985.

Johnston, Basil, *Ojibway Ceremonies*. Toronto: Mc-Clelland and Stewart, 1982.

Jonaitis, Aldona, *Art of the Northern Tlingit*. Seattle: University of Washington Press, 1989.

Josephy, Alvin M., Jr., ed., *The American Heritage Book of Indians*. New York: American Heritage/ Bonanza Books, 1988.

Kinietz, W. Vernon, *The Indians of the Western Great Lakes: 1615-1760*. Ann Arbor: University of Michigan Press, 1991.

Kirk, R., *Tradition & Change on the Northwest Coast*. Seattle: University of Washington Press, 1986.

Koch, Ronald P., *Dress Clothing of the Plains Indians*. Norman: University of Oklahoma Press, 1977.

Krause, Aurel, *The Tlingit Indians*. Transl. by Erna Gunther. Seattle: University of Washington Press, 1956.

Kroeber, C. B., and B. L. Fontana, *Massacre on the Gila*. Tucson: University of Arizona Press, 1986.

Laubin, Reginald, and Gladys Laubin, *Indian Dances of North America: Their Importance to Indian Life*. Norman: University of Oklahoma Press, 1977.

Lowie, Robert H.:
The Crow Indians. Lincoln: University of Nebraska Press, 1963.
Indians of the Plains. Lincoln: University of Nebraska Press, 1982.

McClintock, Walter, *The Old North Trail*. Lincoln: University of Nebraska Press, 1968.

Mails, Thomas E.:
Dog Soldiers, Bear Men and Buffalo Women. Englewood Cliffs, N.J.: Prentice-Hall, 1973.
The Mystic Warriors of the Plains. New York: Mallard Press, 1991.
The People Called Apache. Englewood Cliffs, N.J.: Prentice-Hall, 1974.

Malone, Patrick M., *The Skulking Way of War*. Lanham, Md.: Madison Books, 1991.

Maxwell, James A., ed., *America's Fascinating Indian Heritage*. Pleasantville, N.Y.: Reader's Digest Association, 1978.

Melody, Michael E., *The Apache*. New York: Chelsea House Publishers, 1988.

Members of the Potomac Corral of the Westerners, Washington, D.C., *Great Western Indian Fights*. Lincoln: University of Nebraska Press, 1960.

Murie, James R., *Ceremonies of the Pawnee*. Ed. by Douglas R. Parks. Lincoln: University of Nebraska Press, 1981.

Nabokov, Peter, ed., *Testimony*. New York: Viking Penguin, 1991.

Niethammer, Carolyn, *Daughters of the Earth*. New York: MacMillan, 1977.

Opler, Morris Edward, *An Apache Life-Way*. New York: Cooper Square Publishers, 1965.

Ortiz, Alfonso, ed., *Southwest*. Vol. 10 of *Handbook of North American Indians*. Washington, D.C.: Smithsonian Institution, 1983.

Owen, Roger C., James J. F. Deetz, and Anthony D. Fisher, eds., *The North American Indians*. New York: MacMillan, 1967.

Paul, Doris A., *The Navajo Code Talkers*. Bryn Mawr, Pa.: Dorrance, 1973.

Peckham, Howard H., *Captured by Indians*. New Brunswick, N.J.: Rutgers University Press, 1954.

Penney, David W., ed., *Art of the American Indian Frontier: The Chandler-Pohrt Collection*. Seattle: University of Washington Press, 1992.

Peterson, Harold L., *Arms and Armor in Colonial America*. New York: Bramhall House, 1956.

Pond, Samuel W., *The Dakota or Sioux in Minnesota As They Were in 1834*. St. Paul: Minnesota Historical Society Press, 1986.

Powers, William K., *Oglala Religion*. Lincoln: University of Nebraska Press, 1977.

Rabineau, Phyllis, *Feather Arts*. Chicago: Field Museum of Natural History, 1979.

Ray, Verne F., *Primitive Pragmatists*. Seattle: University of Washington Press, 1963.

Roe, Frank Gilbert, *The Indian and the Horse*. Norman: University of Oklahoma Press, 1955.

Russell, Carl P., *Guns On the Early Frontiers*. New York: Bonanza Books, 1957.

Russell, Howard S., *Indian New England before the Mayflower*. Hanover, N.H.: University Press of New England, 1980.

Schultz, James Willard, *Recently Discovered Tales of Life among the Indians*. Ed. by Warren L. Hanna. Missoula, Mont.: Mountain Press, 1988.

Schulze-Thulin, Axel, ed., *Indianer der Prärien und Plains*. Stuttgart: Linden Museum, 1987.

Scoouwa: James Smith's Indian Captivity Narrative. Columbus: Ohio Historical Society, 1978.

Spence, Lewis, *The Myths of the North American Indians*. New York: Dover Publications, 1989.

Spencer, Robert F., et al., *The Native Americans*. New York: Harper & Row, 1977.

Spier, Leslie, *Yuman Tribes of the Gila River*. New York: Cooper Square Publishers, 1970.

Stands In Timber, John, and Margot Liberty, *Cheyenne Memories*. Lincoln: University of Nebraska Press, 1967.

Suttles, Wayne, ed., *Northwest Coast*. Vol. 7 of *Handbook of North American Indians*. Washington, D.C.: Smithsonian Institution, 1990.

Taylor, Colin, *The Warriors of the Plains*. New York: Arco, 1975.

Thom, Laine, *Becoming Brave*. San Francisco: Chronicle Books, 1992.

Thomas, Davis, and Karin Ronnefeldt, eds., *People of the First Man*. New York: E. P. Dutton, 1976.

Thwaites, R. G., ed., *Early Western Travels*. Vols. 23 and 24. Cleveland: Arthur H. Clark, 1906.

Trenton, Patricia, and Patrick T. Houlihan, *Native Americans*. New York: Harry N. Abrams, 1989.

Trigger, B. G., *The Children of Aataentsic*. Kingston, Ontario: McGill-Queen's University Press, 1987.

Underhill, Ruth Moore, *Red Man's America*. Chicago: University of Chicago Press, 1971.

VanDerBeets, Richard, ed., *Held Captive by Indians*. Knoxville: University of Tennessee Press, 1973.

Vangen, Roland Dean, *Indian Weapons*. Palmer Lake, Colo.: Filter Press, 1972.

Vestal, S., *Warpath*. Boston: Houghton Mifflin, 1934.

Viola, Herman J., *After Columbus*. Washington, D.C.: Smithsonian Books, 1990.

Walker, James R., *Lakota Belief and Ritual*. Ed. by Raymond J. DeMallie, and Elaine A. Jahner. Lincoln: University of Nebraska Press, 1991.

Wallace, Anthony F. C., *The Death and Rebirth of the Seneca*. New York: Alfred A. Knopf, 1970.

Walters, Anna Lee, *The Spirit of Native America*. San Francisco: Chronicle Books, 1989.

Weatherford, Jack, *Native Roots*. New York: Crown Publishers, 1991.

Webb, Walter Prescott, *The Great Plains*. Lincoln: University of Nebraska Press, 1959.

White, Jon Manchip, *Everyday Life of the North American Indian*. New York: Holmes & Meier Publishers, 1979.

Wilbur, C. Keith, *The New England Indians*. Chester, Conn.: Globe Pequot Press, 1978.

Wildschut, William, *Crow Indian Medicine Bundles*. Ed. by John C. Ewers. New York: Museum of the American Indian, 1975.

Williams, Samuel Cole, *Adair's History of the American Indians*. New York: Promontory Press, 1930.

Wissler, Clark, *Indians of the United States*. New York: Anchor Books, 1966.

PERIODICALS

Cleland, Charles F., "Yuma Dolls." *American Indian Art Magazine*, May 1980.

Hale, Duane K., "Uncle Sam's Warriors." *Chronicles of Oklahoma*, Winter 1992.

Holm, Tom:
"Culture, Ceremonialism, and Stress." *Armed Forces & Society*, Winter 1986.
"Intergenerational Rapprochement among American Indians." *Journal of Political and Military Sociology*, Spring 1984.
"Legacy of American Indian Participation in World War II." *The Stars and Stripes*, June 14, 1984.

McCoy, Ronald, "Circles of Power." *Plateau* (Flagstaff, Ariz.), 1984.

Mitchell, Donald, "Predatory Warfare, Social Status, and the North Pacific Slave Trade." *Ethnology*, January 1984.

Newcomb, W. W., Jr., "A Re-examination of the Causes of Plains Warfare." *American Anthropologist*, 1950, Vol. 52.

Starr, Michael L., "She Did Not Lead a Movement." *American History Illustrated*, August 1980.

Stewart, K. M., "Mohave Warfare." *Southwestern Journal of Anthropology*, November 3, 1947.

Swadesh, Morris, "Motivations in Nootka Warfare." *Southwestern Journal of Anthropology*, Spring 1948.

OTHER PUBLICATIONS

Haynie, Nancy Anne, ed., "Native Americans and the Military." U.S. Army Forces Command Public Affairs. Fort McPherson, Ga.: March 1984.

"Indians in the War: Burial of a Brave." Pamphlet. Washington, D.C.: U.S. Department of the Interior, Office of Indian Affairs, November 1945.

"Ledger Art of the Crow and Gros Ventre Indians: 1879-1897." Catalog. Billings, Mont.: Yellowstone Art Center, 1985.

Meadows, W. C., "Tonkonga." Master's Thesis. Norman: University of Oklahoma, 1991.

"Native American Veterans." Statistical Brief. Washington, D.C.: Veterans Administration, October 1985.

"Sacred Circles." Catalog. Kansas City, Mo.: Nelson Gallery of Art, Atkins Museum of Fine Arts, 1977.

"Treasures of the Lowie Museum." Catalog. Berkeley: Robert H. Lowie Museum of Anthropology, University of California, 1968.

Williams, Jack S., and Robert L. Hoover, "Arms of the Apacheria." *Occasional Publications in Anthropology, Ethnology Series*, No. 44. Paper. Greeley: University of Northern Colorado, 1983.

PICTURE CREDITS

The sources for the illustrations that appear in this book are listed below. Credits from left to right are separated by semicolons, from top to bottom by dashes.

Cover: Charles H. Barstow Collection, Eastern Montana College Library, Special Collections, Billings. **6:** Library of Congress, USZ62-106370. **7:** Library of Congress, USZ62-61750. **8:** National Anthropological Archives (NAA), Smithsonian Institution, no. 617. **9:** Seaver Center for Western History Research, Natural History Museum of Los Angeles County. **10:** NAA, Smithsonian Institution, no. 1426-A. **11:** Library of Congress, USZ62-102872. **12, 13:** Library of Congress. **14, 15:** NAA, Smithsonian Institution, nos. 54879; 2023. **16:** Library of Congress, USZ62-53756. **17:** NAA, Smithsonian Institution, no. 76-13379. **18:** National Museum of Natural History (NMNH), Smithsonian Institution, photo courtesy Joslyn Art Museum, Omaha, Nebraska. **20:** Map by Maryland Carto-Graphics, Inc. **22, 23:** Arizona State Museum, University of Arizona, photo Helga Teiwes, C-16742—Museum für Volkerkunde, Staatliche Museen Preussischer Kulturbesitz, Berlin, photo Dietrich Graf. **25:** Ed Brennan, courtesy *American Indian Art Magazine*. **26, 27:** © Jack W. Dykinga. **29:** David W. Vaughan. **30:** Jean-Loup Charmet, Paris. **34, 35:** Werner Forman Archive, London; from the collection of the Gilcrease Museum, Tulsa, Oklahoma. **37:** Library of Congress. **38:** Courtesy Royal Ontario Museum, Toronto, Canada. **39:** Werner Forman Archive, London/Field Museum of Natural History, Chicago. **40, 41:** Courtesy Royal British Columbia Museum, Victoria, B.C. **42:** Addison Doty, courtesy Morning Star Gallery. **43:** NAA, Smithsonian Institution, no. 76-4731. **44:** National Museum of the American Indian (NMAI), Smithsonian Institution, photo Karen Furth. **45:** Werner Forman Archive, London/NMAI, Smithsonian Institution. **47:** Smithsonian Institution, no. 3413A—Charles H. Barstow Collection, Eastern Montana College Library, Special Collections, Billings, photo Michael Crummett. **48, 49:** Charles H. Barstow Collection, Eastern Montana College Library, Special Collections, Billings, photo Michael Crummett. **51:** Southwest Museum, MCC.208, Los Angeles. **52:** The Detroit Institute of Arts, Founders Society Purchase with funds from Flint Ink Corporation, photo Robert Hensleigh. **53:** Courtesy Colorado Historical Society. **54:** Joslyn Art Museum, Omaha, Nebraska. **57:** Denver Art Museum, acc. no. 1947.181. **58:** Peabody Museum, Harvard University, photo Hillel Burger, T1235c—Smithsonian Institution, no. 129832. **59:** Buffalo Bill Historical Center, NA 203.357, gift of Mr. and Mrs. Richard A. Pohrt; Denver Art Museum, acc. no. 1938.265. **60:** Cranbrook Institute of Science, 3146—The Behring-Hofmann Educational Institute, courtesy Phoebe Apperson Hearst Museum, University of California at Berkeley; Peabody Museum, Harvard University, photo Hillel Burger, T1273ii. **61:** Colter Bay Indian Arts Museum, Grand Teton National Park, Wyoming, photo John Odenkamp and Cynthia Sabransky. **62:** Denver Art Museum, acc. no. 1936.350; Buffalo Bill Historical Center, NA 203.347, gift of Mr. and Mrs. Richard A. Pohrt. **63:** University Museum Archives, University of Pennsylvania, neg. no. T4-402—from the collection of the Gilcrease Museum, Tulsa, Oklahoma. **64:** Buffalo Bill Historical Center, NA 203.354, gift of Mr. and Mrs. Richard A. Pohrt. **65:** Horn Headdress: Osage, dyed horsehair, dyed feathers, bird skin, hide, glass beads, fur, horn, silk, wool, cotton, and sinew. The Brooklyn Museum 11.694.9050, Museum Expedition 1911, Museum Collection Fund; © The Detroit Institute of Arts, funds from State of Michigan, City of Detroit and Founders Society—courtesy Thomas Burke Memorial Washington State Museum, cat. no. 2452, photo Eduardo Calderón. **66:** Joslyn Art Museum, Omaha, Nebraska. **67:** Linden-Museum Stuttgart, photos Ursula Didoni. **68, 69:** Joslyn Art Museum, Omaha, Nebraska; Linden-Museum Stuttgart, photo Ursula Didoni. **70, 71:** Linden-Museum Stuttgart, photos Ursula Didoni. **72:** Rare Books and Manuscripts Division, The New York Public Library, Astor, Lenox and Tilden Foundations, photo Paulus Leeser; Joslyn Art Museum, Omaha, Nebraska. **73:** Joslyn Art Museum, Omaha, Nebraska. **74:** Denver Art Museum, acc. no. 1947.259. **76, 77:** Library of Congress, USZ62-101269. **78, 79:** Craig Chesek/American Museum of Natural History, neg. no. 4704(1). **80:** American Museum of Natural History, courtesy The Minnesota Historical Society. **81:** Joslyn Art Museum, Omaha, Nebraska. **82:** Christopher C. Stotz, Archives and Manuscripts Division of the Oklahoma Historical Society, photo. no. 3653; NAA, Smithsonian Institution, no. 56961. **84, 85:** National Museum of American Art, Washington, D.C./Art Resource, New York. **86:** NAA, Smithsonian Institution, no. 53401-A. **87:** © Jerry Jacka, courtesy Colter Bay Indian Arts Museum, Grand Teton National Park, Wyoming. **88:** Smithsonian Institution, no. 201154. **90, 91:** Joslyn Art Museum, Omaha, Nebraska. **93:** From *Shadows on Glass: The Indian World of Ben Wittick* by Patricia Janis Broder, Rowman and Littlefield, Savage, Maryland, 1990. **94:** NAA, Smithsonian Institution, no. 4129B. **95:** Smithsonian Institution, no. 263122. **97:** Peabody Museum, Harvard University, photo Hillel Burger, no. T942. **98:** Collection of the Glenbow, Calgary, Alberta, AF3974; Smithsonian Institution, no. 165859. **99:** Craig Chesek/American Museum of Natural History, neg. no. 4705(1); © Jerry Jacka, courtesy Colter Bay Indian Arts Museum, Grand Teton National Park, Wyoming. **100:** Denver Art Museum, acc. no. 1964.288. **101:** Smithsonian Institution, MS 39-B. **102:** Arizona Historical Society. **105:** Ben Benschneider. **106:** Library of Congress, USZ62-58914. **108, 109:** University Museum Archives, University of Pennsylvania, neg. no. S4-140726. **110, 111:** Milton Snow/courtesy Navajo Nation Museum (N07-41); photo Larry Sherer, courtesy George H. Kirk. **112, 113:** State Historical Society of Wisconsin—National Archives, neg. no. 111-B-26; Library of Congress, B-8171-2746—General Sweeny's Museum, Republic, Missouri. **114, 115:** Museum of New Mexico, neg. no. 2114; courtesy Nebraska State Historical Society—National Museum of American History, Smithsonian Institution, photo Henry Beville. **116, 117:** Grant Wilson; National Archives, neg. no. 111-SC-48488—Larry Sherer, medal courtesy Choctaw Nation of Oklahoma; U.S. Army Signal Museum, Ft. Gordon, Georgia. **118, 119:** National Archives; UPI/Bettmann—Larry Sherer, insignia courtesy Institute of Heraldry, Alexandria, Virginia. **120-125:** William C. Meadows. **126, 127:** Dan O'Boyle (U.S. Army). **128, 129:** Linden-Museum Stuttgart, photo Ursula Didoni—National Museum of American Art, Washington, D.C./Art Resource, New York. **131:** Library of Congress, USZ62-77107. **132, 133:** Courtesy the Trustees of the British Museum, London. **136, 137:** Library of Congress, USZ62-2736—Canadian Museum of Civilization, neg. no. 892-4660. **138:** Anne S. K. Brown Military Collection, Brown University Library, Providence, Rhode Island. **140:** Larry Sherer, courtesy David Condon, Inc. **142:** Library of Congress. **143:** Richardson's *Arctic Searching Expedition*, 1851, from Hudson's Bay Company Archives, Provincial Archives of Manitoba. **145:** NAA, Smithsonian Institution, no. 43848-E—courtesy NMNH, Smithsonian Institution, from the exhibition *Crossroads of Continents: Cultures of Siberia and Alaska*. **146, 147:** Courtesy the collections of the Museum of Anthropology and Ethnology, St. Petersburg, Russia, except bottom left, courtesy NMNH, Smithsonian Institution, all from the exhibition *Crossroads of Continents: Cultures of Siberia and Alaska*. **148:** Courtesy NMNH, Smithsonian Institution, from the exhibition *Crossroads of Continents: Cultures of Siberia and Alaska*. **150:** Peabody Museum, Harvard University, photo Hillel Burger, T1261a. **151:** NAA, Smithsonian Institution, no. 83-7794. **152, 153:** NAA, Smithsonian Institution, no. 79-3858. **154, 155:** Ben Benschneider, courtesy South Dakota State Historical Society. **157:** NAA, Smithsonian Institution, no. 83-7759. **158:** Werner Forman Archive, London/Smithsonian Institution. **159:** Denver Art Museum, acc. no. 1960.129.3. **160, 161:** National Museum of American Art, Washington, D.C./Art Resource, New York. **162:** University Museum Archives, University of Pennsylvania, neg. no. T4-416. **165-177:** Backgrounds from *The Vanishing Race: The Last Great Indian Council*, photos Joseph K. Dixon on the Rodman Wanamaker expedition, published by Doubleday, New York, 1913. **165:** American Museum of Natural History, courtesy The Minnesota Historical Society. **166, 167:** Addison Doty, courtesy Morning Star Gallery—Salamander Books Limited, London/Smithsonian Institution; Linden-Museum Stuttgart, photo Ursula Didoni. **168, 169:** Frank Lerner, American Museum of Natural History—courtesy NMNH, Smithsonian Institution, from the exhibition *Crossroads of Continents: Cultures of Siberia and Alaska*—Buffalo Bill Historical Center, NA 108.95, photo © Robert Hensleigh—Smithsonian Institution, no. 233109. **170, 171:** Linden-Museum Stuttgart, photo Ursula Didoni—Lee Boltin/American Museum of Natural History; Cranbrook Institute of Science, 3691; courtesy NMNH, Smithsonian Institution, from the exhibition *Crossroads of Continents: Cultures of Siberia and Alaska*. **172, 173:** Smithsonian Institution, no. 381474—Buffalo Bill Historical Center, Chandler-Pohrt Collection, gift of The Pilot Foundation—C. M. Dixon, Canterbury, Kent/Smithsonian Institution. **174, 175:** Richard and Marion Pohrt (974), photo © Robert Hensleigh; Musée de l'Homme, Paris, photo M. Delaplanche; courtesy NMNH, Smithsonian Institution, from the exhibition *Crossroads of Continents: Cultures of Siberia and Alaska*—Linden-Museum Stuttgart, photo Ursula Didoni—Werner Forman Archive, London, courtesy Museum für Volkerkunde, Staatliche Museen Preussischer Kulturbesitz, Berlin. **176, 177:** Smithsonian Institution, no. 384119—Denver Art Museum, acc. no. 1938.158; Buffalo Bill Historical Center, NA 102.87, photo © Dirk Bakker.